Time-Limited Counselling

PROFESSIONAL SKILLS FOR COUNSELLORS

The *Professional Skills for Counsellors* series, edited by Colin Feltham, covers the practical, technical and professional skills and knowledge which trainee and practising counsellors need to improve their competence in key areas of therapeutic practice.

Titles in the series include:

Time-Limited Counselling

Colin Feltham

SAGE Publications
London • Thousand Oaks • New Delhi

© Colin Feltham 1997

This edition first published 1997

SAGE Publications Ltd
6 Bonhill Street
London EC2A 4PU

SAGE Publications Inc.
2455 Teller Road
Thousand Oaks, California 91320

SAGE Publications India Pvt Ltd
32, M-Block Market
Greater Kailash – I
New Delhi 110 048

British Library Cataloguing in Publication data

A catalogue record for this book is available
from the British Library.

ISBN 0 8039 7974 6
ISBN 0 8039 7975 4 (pbk)

Library of Congress catalog record available

Typeset by Mayhew Typesetting, Rhayader, Powys
Printed in Great Britain by Hartnolls Ltd, Bodmin, Cornwall

'We must use time as a tool, not as a couch.'

John F. Kennedy

'And he that will not apply New Remedies,
must expect New Evils: for Time is the
greatest *Innovateur*.'

Francis Bacon (*Essay XXIII: Of Innovations*)

For
Eileen and Stan Feltham
whose lives were sadly short and limited

Contents

Acknowledgements

Many people helped by giving information, accounts of their experiences and by responding to my survey, and I am very grateful to them all (unfortunately too many to name). Colleagues from various agencies including Mentors Counselling Consultants have been particularly helpful. I am grateful to Graham Curtis Jenkins, Carol Mohamed and Peter Roberts for supplying me with helpful texts. Particular thanks also go to those people who have allowed me to use their stories.

Jason Aronson Inc. for permission to reproduce Table 5.1 from *Techniques of Brief Psychotherapy* by Walter Flegenheimer (1982).

Guilford Publications Inc. for permission to reproduce Table 2.1 from *Theory and Practice of Brief Therapy*, by S.H. Budman and A.S. Gurman (1988).

The Krishnamurti Foundation Ltd for permission to reproduce *Psychotherapists in Dialogue with Krishnamurti*, a 1975 Conference Report (Appendix 1).

Dr Anthony Ryle for permission to reproduce *The Psychotherapy File* (Appendix 2). This is part of the procedure of Cognitive Analytic Therapy but its use here is acknowledged to be quite distinct from CAT.

1

Introduction: the Nature of Time

Some explanation for the title of this book is called for at the outset. Since my own view is that counselling and psychotherapy are largely synonymous, the title could as well be 'Time-Limited Psychotherapy'. It is not titled 'Brief Therapy' because, although I will mainly refer to quite short-term therapy and counselling, 'brief' in the context of psychotherapy tends to refer to both counselling by design and counselling by default and has been used to refer to anything up to 40 or 50 sessions. Time-limited counselling, for the purposes of this book, mainly refers to therapeutic counselling which is usually designed to be of a pre-determined number of sessions, usually not more than 20 at most, and including single session therapy. In agencies where actual limits are set – for example, by employee assistance programmes or American Health Maintenance Organizations (HMOs) – the number is usually between about 6 and 20 (see also Barten, 1971). This book takes individual counselling as its focus but many issues are transferable to work in other therapeutic modalities or arenas. (See Freeman (1990) on couple counselling; Budman (1981) on group therapy; de Shazer (1991), Boscolo and Bertrando (1993) on family therapy.)

Having said this, I must now alert readers to my belief that effective time-limited counselling, indeed all counselling, benefits from an exploration of its temporal assumptions. A major assumption in this book – and in many brief therapy approaches – is that time is both a linear affair in which our familiar personal narratives are embedded and, simultaneously, an illusion behind which lies the ever-present possibility of many different ways forward. Counselling that is time-sensitive is a pragmatic venture but also raises the fundamental question of how we understand time – how it shapes our problems and solutions. Whitrow (1988) has discussed the rival concepts of duration and instant, and this is an excellent way of understanding the tension existing in counselling that is sensitive to the use of time. We have expected therapy to be a somewhat extended process but simultaneously we know that dramatic breakthroughs and unexpected endings may happen at any time in the process.

Time-limited counselling is not, in my view, a hurried and superficial activity – as its critics like to suggest – but is simply one way of doing counselling differently, based on questions about the meaning and use of time, and the aims and scope of counselling and therapy. Readers may note that time-limited counselling can be rendered as TLC which also stands for tender loving care. I have avoided using TLC in the text but I believe that as much tender loving care can be conveyed in brief as in lengthy therapy! Certainly, time-limited counselling as a title has some problems, connoting as it does perhaps a sense of negativity and shortage. Some writers prefer to speak of time-sensitive therapy or time-efficient therapy; Elton Wilson (1996) has coined the term 'time-conscious psychological therapy'. We might try time-centred counselling, time-informed therapy or, simply, timed counselling but none of these feels wholly satisfactory. 'Counselling based on an awareness of time factors, including consideration of therapeutically optimal temporal dosage' perhaps captures the essence of it.

Let us now look briefly at some of the universal issues contained within the concept of time, so that we can then proceed to ask what temporal assumptions are embedded within the concepts of mental health and dysfunction, human development, problem solving and personal growth. Even as you read this, you may be aware of your own attitudes towards time and its use: do you read the text in a leisurely or hurried way, in a methodical linear manner, or do you skip certain sections to get to what seems most useful to you? Do you read it in one sitting or over many weeks?

What is time?

For most of us time means the daily passing of morning, afternoon, evening and night; it entails a sequence of events and a sense of past, present and future; we may think of our lives in terms of a linear narrative between birth and death, and of history as a linear progression. Time is measured by the clock and calendar so that we know what to expect at certain times, when to be somewhere and how long we have got. Time seems to be ubiquitous, taken for granted, as the medium in which we live; time seems to move ever forward, naturally and without needing to be examined. Yet philosophers, theologians, physicists, biologists, anthropologists, poets and others have puzzled over what it really means, whether it really exists and what the relationship is between our subjective sense of time and what time might objectively be.

It does not take much thought to realise the illusory or problematic nature of time: the past, now gone, no longer exists, except as memory traces; the future, always still to come, doesn't yet exist, except as anticipation; we might say, then, that the past and future have no objective reality, existing only in our minds as memory and expectation. That leaves only the present. Yet what is the present except a fine dividing line between past and future, and exactly what reality does this fine line have? From a historical perspective, the present may be defined as the late twentieth century (although this historical structuring of time may itself be regarded as entirely arbitrary). From the personal perspective, the present may be defined as this year in my life, this week or day. The now in which I write this is over, however, as soon as it is mentioned and the moment in which you read this is sometime in the future (from my now), yet it will be in your present that you read it, many months or years after I have written it. Where the writer and each reader of this book is 'coming from' – in terms of our exact interests in time-limited work, our individual histories and psychological differences, theoretical orientations, and so on – colours our understanding of the text and its subject matter. This almost inevitable temporal imbroglio has serious conflictual effects in human relationships, as family therapists know (Boscolo and Bertrando, 1993).

If you have any difficulty or frustration considering the elusive concept of time, you are in good company. Hawking (1988) attempts to understand and explain the origins of time with reference to the Big Bang and black holes. Coveney and Highfield (1991) examine the physicists' and biologists' preoccupations with time, focusing on the notion that time, whatever it is, is clearly irreversible. Shallis (1983) explores scientific, mystical and subjective elements of time. Physicist David Bohm commended a dialogue between science and mysticism, and regarded human thought as the mechanism responsible for the creation of the illusions of time and all personal and social problems (Krishnamurti and Bohm, 1985). Post-modernist social theorist Baudrillard (1994) challenges the concept of the purposeful linearity of time on a historical scale. Adam (1995), writing from social and feminist theory perspectives, urges us to make consideration of time central to social analysis.

Thomas (1991), calling on mystical, musical, bioenergetic and Jungian concepts, argues that a radical analysis of time is necessary to the development of true human potential. Rawlence (1985) has presented many fascinating views on time, including factors of gender difference in perception of time, the meaning of rites and holidays, and so on. Graham (1990) weaves together the concepts of time and energy in her examination of health and complementary medicine. Counsellors and psychotherapists have until recently shown little zest for analysing time, but McGrath and Kelly (1986) have looked at the social psychology of time and Slife (1993) examines time from the perspective of theoretical and philosophical psychology, with some reference to psychotherapy and its temporal assumptions.

While cyclical time was and still is taken for granted by Hindus and others, the Judaeo-Christian tradition has always promoted a view of linear and directed time. Other traditions have sometimes argued for the coexistence of at least two modes of time; the ancient Iranians, for example, recognised both an indivisible time (a creative, eternal now) and the time of the long dominion which brought decay and death (Whitrow, 1988). The discrepancies between concepts of reincarnation and one earthly life followed by either a heavenly eternity or eternal damnation must also be contrasted with the existentialist view that each human life is purely and simply the 70 or 80 years that it usually is, without survival, repetition or mystery. Statistics available to us now suggest that Western men can normally expect to live into their 70s and women into their 80s. Not so long ago, however, life expectancy was considerably shorter. Obviously the culture and era in which we live influences our perception of time and the way in which we use time. Other factors also affect how we perceive time: if you have a terminal illness, time may be very precious; if you are in prison time will drag and hang heavily on you; and so on.

The notion of time schedules and punctuality has been traced to the original Benedictine monks, for whom each day was passed in a strictly accountable, efficient way (Adam, 1995). The Industrial Revolution too emphasised schedules and erected artificial boundaries between times of work, rest and holiday. Psychoanalysis helped to promote the importance of punctuality, not only as a convenience but also as a marker of commitment or resistance to treatment. Insofar as time is money and efficiency, we seem in the West to be inescapably hooked into time schedules, appointments, deadlines and the accompanying stress. A combination of contemporary hurry sickness, uncritical attachment to clock time and alienation from natural body rhythms has led to physical illness as well as psychological ailments (Adam, 1992). American psychotherapist Kottler (1993) argues that Latin cultures have greater respect for the present. Hence, in Peru Kottler reports experiencing among his students a healthy, almost complete, disregard for punctuality.

The invention of the pendulum clock in 1657 ensured that time could be accurately tracked. Time is plastic; it can be and has been changed overnight by government decree. Our language is full of references to time: time flies, time drags, time is money, time and tide wait for no one, time heals, only time will tell, there's no time like the present. We say that we have a lot of time for someone, or no time at all, meaning that we do or do not like and respect them. We often have certain unexamined assumptions about how long things should or do take. How long does it take to build a house, to sell a house, to write a book, to learn a language? Members of certain religious organisations have been known to build a church in a weekend. Although property conveyancing in Britain often takes months, when necessary it can happen in a matter of hours. It is not only at novel-writing competitions, where complete novels are written in 24 hours, that creative speed is exhibited. Stephen King wrote his novel *The Running Man* in 72 hours; Samuel Johnson wrote the novel *Rasselas* in the evening of one week in 1759. Various television shows have demonstrated how much can be achieved within, say, 48 hours, such as the conversion of a derelict building into a playcentre or the transportation of animals across continents and the building of humane living quarters for them. Whatever the motivating factors, there is evidence that our assumptions are based on a norm that can be challenged.

Temporal assumptions in the psychological world may need as much challenging as assumptions about time requirements in the physical world. It has been said that nothing lasts, neither tragedy nor triumph. Our problems themselves do not last forever, and neither do our solutions. We are currently seeing through the pseudo-triumph of much high-dose (long-term) psychotherapy and turning our attention to low-dose, time-limited counselling and therapy. We might try to remember that today's attempted solutions will themselves not last forever and that probably there is a time for time-limited counselling and a time for long-term counselling. While we are considering this issue, we might at least fleetingly give attention to the place time has in the way we construct our human problems and attempt to overcome them, although this larger question is mainly outside the scope of the present book.

2

Attitudes to Time in Counselling and Psychotherapy

It is important to consider quite broadly clients' and counsellors' attitudes to time, how time is used, how it might be better used, which aspects of time may be negotiable or non-negotiable, and what time means for personal problem solving or personal growth.

Aspects of developmental psychology

Certain aspects of human development are beyond dispute. Pregnancies, for example, normally last about nine months. The human infant is vulnerable, cannot fend for itself and needs to be fed, cleaned and cared for for a considerable time. Most germane to our discussion are questions about the timing of developmental changes and malfunctions. Most counsellors would agree that a great deal of our habitual behaviour – comprised of our scripts, our defences and so on – is laid down in the earliest years of life. Many believe that the earlier we suffer traumas and deprivations, and the more of these events we suffer, the greater the impact these have on us and the harder they are to change, even within therapy later in life. There are differences of opinion about the degree of freedom of choice we had as children (to react one way or another to adversity, for example) and the extent to which behaviour stemming from childhood is reversible. Even within the psychoanalytic tradition there are differences of opinion about the extent to which we are afflicted by innate drives and the conflicts between them as opposed to damaging ruptures in early relationships.

The picture is complicated still more by the fact that some therapists (and millions of Hindus and Buddhists) believe that many of our problems stem from experiences in previous lives. Certain Jungians, for example, practise a form of past lives therapy which aims to acquaint people with, or liberate them from, the detrimental effects of ignorant acts or accidents in previous incarnations (Woolger, 1990). However sceptical you may be about this (and you may not be sceptical at all), it introduces a wholly different timescale into our discussion. The prospect of future incarnations, too, affects the way in which we interpret our lives (and our clients' lives) now.

If you believe that adult life is largely predetermined by the events, circumstances and ravages of childhood, this is quite different from believing that adulthood, and indeed mid-life and old age, present not only crisis points but also immense opportunities and freedoms of their own. Remember too that our perceptions of time often alter according to our stage of life. Thus, Brundage and Mackeracher (1980) argue that children and young adults measure their lives from birth to the present, while those aged about 40 or over are inclined to measure time as something left before death. Rowe (1994) does not share this rather gloomy view of the latter half of life. Each of us decides to what extent we regard life as a repetition of early conflicts, as a series of exciting new stages, or as a perpetual blank page. Also, certain debates remain unresolved about periodicity in human life. Are astrological influences at work which affect our development? Are seasonal affective disorder and premenstrual syndrome real, imagined or not yet fully understood? There may be some facts of human development but there are opinions and choices too. There is even the view that developmental psychology itself rests on mythical foundations (Morss, 1995).

Lifespan psychologists may be confounded by exceptional cases. The following case illustrates humorously how our best-founded expectations can sometimes be way off. It was reported in 1995 that the world's oldest woman, Jeanne Calment of Arles, France, was 120 years old and still going strong. When she was 90, a lawyer had offered to pay her rent for the rest of her life on condition that he inherited her house when she died. He was at that time 47 years old and had, therefore, made a reasonable (apparently rock-solid) bet. In fact he died, aged 77, in 1995, having paid more than three times the value of the house. If there is any moral for therapists in this wonderful story, it may be that we should never totally rely on our usual lifespan expectations and always leave room for surprises.

Consider, too, contrary to our conditioned tendency to dwell on negative early experiences, the impact of *positive* earlier experiences. A man who had a religious experience spoke of it in these words: 'The vision lasted a few seconds and was gone; but the memory of it and the sense of the reality of it has remained during the quarter of a century which has since elapsed' (Happold, 1963: 136). Many people who have been subjected to near death experiences report that they retain a vivid memory of the experience which exerts a powerful positive influence on how they live their lives thereafter. Often a brush with death sensitises people to the precariousness and preciousness of life. In a study of survivors of one maritime disaster it was found that 71 per cent thereafter claimed to live life to the fullest (Joseph et al., 1993). There are of course many Christian texts highlighting the importance of the eternal now or the valuing of the present moment (e.g. Goldsmith, 1965). It can also be argued that early deprivation and suffering is often character-forming. McCord (1978) followed up on the treatment (various kinds of formal social support, including counselling and academic mentoring) of a group of youths after 30 years and found that they compared negatively with an untreated control group in terms of illness, career development, dependency and other factors.

The point I am making here is that there are many interpretations of human development; perhaps too many of them derived from or associated with psychotherapeutic theory emphasise psychopathology and negativity generally. Brief therapists such as Budman and Gurman (1988) present an adult developmental model which challenges this. Elton Wilson (1996) incorporates a life stage rationale into her model of time-conscious psychological therapy. In time-limited counselling the counsellor is bound to consider whether and how his or her favoured theory – and its implications – fits with short-term work.

Psychoanalytic perspectives

While many of Freud's early clinical cases were in fact of very short duration, psychoanalytic theory suggests that therapy must be either temporally indeterminate or long term. According to

Freud unconscious processes are timeless, which means that 'they are not ordered temporally, that time does not change them in any way and that the idea of time cannot be applied to them' (Freud [1920] 1985: 299). What is repressed, in other words, cannot be de-repressed by the passage of time; early conflicts remain intact until dealt with psychoanalytically. Broadly speaking, the Freudian primary processes, governed by the pleasure principle, operate outside of space and time considerations and it is only the secondary processes, governed by the reality principle (concerned with logic and adaptation), that are amenable to temporal pressures and constraints. As Rycroft (1972) points out, psychoanalysis also assumes that many aspects of present life represent past life; in this scheme of things, many if not most client 'presenting problems' are actually manifestations of much earlier, hidden and subtle unconscious conflicts. Thus, developmental stages that have not been successfully negotiated at the appropriate time, re-present themselves inappropriately later. The logic of this classical view is that no meaningful therapeutic work can be done without reference to deep, early, unconscious conflicts. This working through, of course, takes time and challenges the whole notion of short-term therapy (see Feltham, 1995: 44).

Alexander and French (1946) are generally credited with re-introducing seriously the idea of efficient short-term therapy using psychoanalytic methods. Budman and Gurman (1988) speculate that the timing of this development coincided with Freud's death and the relaxation of analytic orthodoxy in 1939, and the needs of war veterans suffering from battle fatigue (Grinker and Spiegel, 1944). At about the same time, attention was being given to survivors of disasters in need of crisis intervention. Combined with these developments, the emergence of early models of humanistic therapy and cognitive–behavioural methods threw up theoretical challenges to psychoanalysis. Health legislation in the USA in the 1960s, too, led to an emphasis on exploring methods of effective short-term treatments. Pioneers of brief psychoanalytic treatment, including Malan, Sifneos and Mann, published accounts of their work in the 1960s and 1970s. The last few decades have witnessed, then, ongoing tension between an analytical model of therapy that is indifferent to time and models which seek directly to take time factors into account.

A psychoanalyst told me that he had seen one patient for '14 years and not a minute wasted'. This partly reflects the need that some clients undoubtedly have for a long, unbroken, dependent, caring relationship with a therapist. But it also reflects the notion that early damage is likely to have led to a lifetime of related problems, many of which may have to be worked through before getting to the meat of early hurts and conflicts. Also reflected is the view that surface changes in clients' behaviour may be relatively easily facilitated but are problematic. Clients often comply with our expectations as part of their defence system: if we wish to see rapid positive results, compliant clients will give these to us, while remaining in inner turmoil (consciously or unconsciously). Clients may indeed make remarkable symptomatic changes in a short time, yet if their underlying dynamics have been left untouched these changes will not be likely to endure. Thus according to this kind of psychoanalytic criticism, attempted truncation of therapy may be deceptive and even ultimately inefficient, since clients will be forced to return for more therapy and may have even learned to be more defensive due to their experiences at the hands of short-term therapists. A major criticism of time-limited counselling is indeed that it may encourage a flight into spurious health and consequently represent a false economy.

Psychoanalysis and its derivatives typically demand a commitment from clients of two years at the very least, but often much longer; and of attendance at least twice a week, but often three, four or five times a week. There is no pressure for results and, indeed, clients may be persuaded not to make any major life changes or decisions during the early stages. It is still often the case that analysts aim to address the entire personality structure of the client rather than specific problematic issues. Yet analysts manage to limit the time of each session to 50 minutes and often justify this on the grounds that it is containing, that it introduces a discipline, a necessary tension and frustration, and so on. In this sense it is clearly not person-centred (clients are not asked how much time they need or whether they may need longer or shorter sessions) but imposes a traditional temporal framework on clients. However, the sheer amount of time given to the task of free association, for example, conveys a sense of timelessness – the client may mentally roam from current crisis to recent events to early childhood experiences and back again to the immediate relationship with the analyst – and the transference which constitutes the affectively charged imposition of the unresolved past on to the present.

Consider one analysand's experience of (brief!) analysis: 'I only did three years in analysis, five times a week – a relatively short time. It was a terribly painful three years. I remember it was like a raw wound, continuous pain. I cried for hours every day for three years' (Dinnage, 1989: 42). It is, of course, also highly significant that many of the humanistic practitioners' (e.g. Perls, Janov) and cognitive–behavioural (e.g. Ellis, Beck) approaches have evolved out of psychoanalytic practitioners' dissatisfaction with the slow results that were forthcoming in their practices. Gustafson (1986) has pointed out too that the intuitive clinical mastery shown by many practitioners in successful brief therapy is easily and repeatedly lost, and argues that only hard-earned conceptual integration can remedy this.

How long does healing take?

'He really should have got over it by now' is a familiar enough refrain. I recall a man whose son had recently killed himself asking if his wife should not have recovered from her acute grief by now (two months after the death). Most of us assume that a decent period of mourning is essential and that to be apparently unperturbed by traumatic events is to be in denial. Tedeschi and Calhoun (1995: 27), however, report on a woman whose husband was killed in a tornado; she returned to work the next day saying that 'life just has to go on'. As Tedeschi and Calhoun put it: 'For some people, then, time is not necessary to heal wounds because there are no wounds to heal – there are simply difficult situations that have been successfully handled.' On the other hand, a woman who had been widowed many years before wrote angrily to a newspaper which had featured views on how long it takes to recover; she remarked that having been with her husband for many, many years, life was not, nor ever could be the same again and she would *always* miss him. Who can say how long healing typically does or should take?

What we can say is that often after about a year, depending on many factors, most people will have recovered fairly well from a bereavement, although in some cases troublesome symptoms like irritability and increased smoking and alcohol consumption may have actually escalated (Stroebe et al., 1993). We also know that anniversaries of deaths and other significant losses are often times to expect crises. We can say that for a majority of people who have suffered a major trauma, after about two years they will be functioning more or less normally again (Tedeschi and Calhoun, 1995). Those working with the after-effects of major catastrophes observe that there is for some victims a pattern of immediate stability (or pseudo-stability), followed 24 or 48 hours later by emotional collapse, followed days later by a reasonable level of adjustment (Seligman, 1975). We know that some psychological maladies are self-limiting. There is evidence, for example, that episodes of depression last on average for 14 weeks, with or without treatment (Healy, 1990: 188), and that some suicidal crises will pass if the person is supported or detained for a week or two (Seligman, 1975). *Very* roughly, then, we can know what to expect in certain cases.

The Jungian, Joseph Redfearn asks how long healing takes. 'How long does it take God, the beloved, the therapist, the enemy to penetrate, shatter, or melt one's hardness, one's defences? How long does it take to grieve, to sorrow, to repent, to find love? A second? A lifetime? Both could be true' (1992: 257). Although this ambiguity hardly helps counsellors to plan particular strategies or impress funders, it does reflect a reality – that change sometimes occurs rapidly and dramatically (faster than we expect) and sometimes laboriously (much more slowly that we would like). In time-limited counselling we need to be open to, and work with, the possibility of rapid change. We need, too, to adapt our responses to people who are not moving rapidly. One response may be to offer clients long-term support or refer them on; but another response is to offer suitably timed, spaced, tailored therapy, if necessary and possible across a long time span.

There is a rule of thumb that cure or significant alleviation of distress is lengthy in proportion to how long the sickness took to develop and/or corresponds to the age of the person. A moderately unhappy student in his early 20s may well require only two or three counselling sessions, for example. It is also claimed by some that change may take only as long as it took for the original trauma or faulty learning to happen (Andreas and Andreas, 1992). In one workshop I ran on time-limited counselling, the following two opposite reports were made by participants. One woman had been treated by short-term behaviour therapy for agoraphobia. This failed, but after five years of psychotherapy she recovered. Another woman had had a snake phobia for many years. Within 15 minutes of neuro-linguistic programming, she was completely cured and has remained free of that phobia.

It is also worth considering the possible preventive effects of relatively short-term counselling. Single sessions of cognitive analytic therapy, for example, have been offered to people hospitalised following serious self-harming episodes. The rationale for this intervention is that self-harmers frequently go on to make further suicidal attempts and that, given the opportunity to gain some understanding and some tools for dealing with distress, the investment of a single three-hour session is well worth while (Cowmeadow, 1995). In a different context, Pugh (1992) argues that brief interventions with bereaved or soon to be bereaved children may have important long-term effects. The lesson here is that a little, well-timed, may sometimes go a long way.

Guarantees of how long successful therapy will take are of course very rare, although American insurers place some pressure on practitioners to achieve results – or cease claiming payments – within a predetermined time span. Scott and Dryden (1996) assert that 90 per cent of panic-beset clients with mild to moderate agoraphobia are typically panic-free after 12 one-hour sessions of cognitive therapy. This compares with 50–55 per cent of clients given relaxation training and only 5 per cent of clients on a waiting list. A one-year follow-up of cognitive therapy clients has confirmed continuing freedom from panic.

Temporal allusions in therapies

It is often heard in Alcoholics Anonymous and related circles that today is the first day of the rest of your life, and that it is wise to live your life (or your 'recovery') one day at a time. Apart from this folklore-like piece of wisdom, one may identify temporal references in many therapeutic systems. Transactional analysis has its time structuring which includes pastiming and rituals. We have looked at psychoanalytic models, and all in one way or another reflect notions of early causation, developmental stages, repetition, the timelessness of unconscious conflict, and so on. Chronically endured pain is a central concept in cognitive analytic therapy. Jungian therapy embraces the notion of synchronicity, where inner and outer realities intersect. Gestalt therapy is very concerned with the here and now, or 'continuous flow'. Behaviour therapy includes the technique of time-out and in most cases builds in assessment concerning onset, duration and severity of symptoms. In cognitive therapy can be found ideas about client's temporal predictions (how long distress has lasted or will last). In personal construct therapy, time-binding refers to the dating of a construct to the time when one formulated it. In NLP a timeline refers to the ways in which we store and process our perceptions of temporal events (James and Woodsmall, 1988).

Existential therapy contains the assertion that behind all present time there is death. When we live authentically in time, knowing ourselves to be mortal, we cannot avoid the sense of time running out and of our lives being our responsibility to create. As Emmy van Deurzen-Smith puts it:

> As simple mortals faced with a limited time to spend in this world, one of the inescapable tasks is to reconcile oneself to having to create a meaningful existence, in which not too much time is wasted and where some sense is made of what could seem nonsensical. (1988: 222)

Somewhat similar sentiments may be found in Frankl (1985), Marteau (1986) and Mann (1973). A connection between very long-term therapy and refusal to accept responsibility for one's imperfect and sometimes painful life is hard to deny.

Many counselling models revolve around the idea of sequential stages of change, including the simple and logical model of beginning, middle and ending stages. Most theories contain some reference to progress and regression, as well as to impasse or being stuck. The concepts of history-taking, time boundaries, timing, pacing, immediacy, presence and termination are common to many therapies. Perhaps the one idea common to *all* counselling orientations is that time does not heal, but certain therapeutic processes must take place. Implicitly, all approaches promise somehow to accelerate change or to improve on the outcome that would be achieved by the un-aided passage of time. (Let us not forget, however, the criticism that the wrong kind of therapy for any one client may actually *delay* improvement.)

Let us remember that time, and clients' temporal attitudes and behaviour, is considered as significant in psychoanalysis as are all other phenomena. Hence the analytic joke: patients who arrive early for their sessions are anxious; those who arrive late are resistant; and those who arrive on time are obsessive!

Objections to time-limited counselling

Time-limited counselling is relatively new, it obviously challenges
many existing traditions of long-term or open-ended therapy, and
it appears to demand that too much thought be given to accountability and results. Clearly it looks as if it is part of the current
political and economic climate of cost-cutting. For some, it
appears to represent opposition to organic notions of time and to
echo mindlessly the prevalent addiction to speed and efficiency
(Adam, 1995).

John Rowan has declared his misgivings about short-term
therapy or counselling, partly because it threatens to short-
change clients, robbing them of the deeper layers of work on
themselves they may need, and partly because it perhaps reflects
the overly cost-conscious mentality of our time and threatens to
overshadow the need for, and the good results often achieved
in, long-term therapy (Rowan, 1993a). But Rowan is also aware
that time saving in therapy has its value. Speaking of the
Enlightenment Intensive (a three-day, Zen-based method of
breaking into higher consciousness), he says 'the Enlightenment
Intensive is a very good experience for getting at an experience
of the Real Self, and anyone who is struggling with (or avoiding)
this issue in therapy would be well advised to go to one. *It
could save them a lot of time*' (Rowan, 1993b: 149; italics added).
Even within transpersonal therapy, then, it is worth considering
whether the client and counsellor use their time to optimal
advantage.

Perhaps the main objection to time-limited therapy is that
change simply takes time, and the kinds of change aimed at by
psychoanalytic practitioners take as long as they must. Thus
Karasu (1992: 282) argues that 'psychotherapy is like a slow-
cooking process that has no microwave substitute'; Karasu
believes that any therapy has its own, sensed time limits which
cannot be prescribed in advance. 'Psychology suggests that in
order to reach the inner recesses of the mind one has to take a
tortuous route. Taking a supposed shortcut will delay the trip; the
therapist may either never get to the destination or miss some
important spots along the way' (Karasu, 1992: 283). Even the most
dedicated of brief therapists will agree with Karasu that *for certain
clients* it would be unrealistic and unethical to arbitrarily curtail
access to needed further therapy.

Bear in mind that all counselling and therapy is time-limited. It is, after all, humanly impossible to dedicate all your time to another human being. Even residential therapists work in shifts, needing their sleep, recreation and private lives. Classical psychoanalysts who see the same patient five times a week for many years are very disciplined about limiting the patient to a 50-minute hour each session. If that is not time-limiting (not to say time-stealing, by a factor of 10 minutes each hour), then what is? Presumably psychoanalysts and other therapists feel justified in sometimes taking long holidays, and believe their clients to be strong enough to manage these breaks. Indeed, an important argument within psychoanalysis and psychoanalytic therapy is that the patient needs a secure frame (which is defined partly by being deprived of endless time) and needs to experience the inevitable absences and unavailability of the therapist. The patient must to some extent fall in with the therapist's convenience, for example he or she can only be seen when other patients are not being seen and when the therapist has no other engagements. Reality factors are always present.

There are many reservations about short-term therapy, some of them very valid. It is clear that some practitioners regard this development with some amusement or irritation as a passing fad; it has even been said that brief psychotherapy resembles a miniaturisation of authentic, long-term psychoanalysis. More examples of problems with and objections to time-limited counselling are given in Chapter 7.

Arguments in favour of time-limited counselling

James Mann put forward one of the most uncompromising and interesting arguments for time-limited psychotherapy:

> Our therapists had no *time* for more patients; patients were in long-term psychotherapy for too long a period of *time*. If it is time that is of the essence, then a time-limited psychotherapy program would be in order. However, since a time-limited psychotherapy still allows for latitude in the use of time, let us then make *time* the issue by defining exactly how long the treatment will take – not twelve treatment hours more or less, but rather exactly twelve treatment hours. If, then, a number of patients were to be treated in twelve treatment interviews offered once or twice each week (in contrast to other kinds of time

distribution), we would have the time variable rather firmly in hand, and we could take the opportunity to study the meaning of time in the treatment of patients in a way not done before. (Mann, 1973: xi–xii)

This statement reflects succinctly a variety of arguments based on economics, realism, research possibilities, clinical issues, and inescapable existential questions. Time as experienced by human beings is finite, it is very definitely a limited resource, yet we try to refuse to accept this fact. Mann suggests that this refusal itself be confronted, both in clinicians and their clients.

Below I outline some of the arguments for time-limited therapeutic work. In many ways these are focused around the historical neglect of time factors by traditional clinicians. Table 2.1 shows one view of the comparisons between short-term and long-term therapists. In becoming interested in working in a time-limited fashion, there is a danger of treating it as a panacea, instead of seeing it as highly applicable at this point in social history in certain cultures, for certain people in certain circumstances. Some have said wisely that short-term therapy should be regarded as a treatment or approach of choice for certain clients, which should coexist with (rather than adversarially seek to oust and replace) longer-term therapy (Rawson, 1992; Coren, 1996).

Economics

Since we are living through an era of management values in which short-term cost-effectiveness, value for money, performance indicators, return on investment, competencies and other buzzwords and business concepts are now commonplace, we might assume that time-limited counselling is simply part of this *Zeitgeist*. In fact many opponents of brief therapy regard it with distaste as having succumbed to just such pressures. American law, insurance and health policies have for some time pushed therapists increasingly into the position of having to justify their work and often to shorten it (Budman and Gurman, 1988). Not all of them have been reluctant, however; Budman and Gurman exhibit an obvious approval and enjoyment of brief therapy. Cummings (1990a) has been one of the most proactive of psychologists in meeting the challenge of value for money in the USA. Although in Britain the pressures on counsellors and therapists are different, practitioners and researchers like Ryle (1990, 1995) and Barkham and Shapiro (1990) have energetically

Table 2.1 *Comparative dominant values of the long-term and short-term therapist*

	Long-term therapist	Short-term therapist
1	Seeks change in basic character.	Prefers pragmatism, parsimony, and least radical intervention, and does not believe in notion of 'cure'.
2	Believes that significant psychological change is unlikely in everyday life.	Maintains an adult developmental perspective from which significant psychological change is viewed as inevitable.
3	Sees presenting problems as reflecting more basic pathology.	Emphasizes patient's strengths and resources; presenting problems are taken seriously (although not necessarily at face value).
4	Wants to 'be there' as patient makes significant changes.	Accepts that many changes will occur 'after therapy' and will not be observable to the therapist.
5	Sees therapy as having a 'timeless' quality and is patient and willing to wait for change.	Does not accept the timelessness of some models of therapy.
6	Unconsciously recognizes the fiscal convenience of maintaining long-term patients.	Fiscal issues often muted, either by the nature of the therapist's practice or by the organizational structure for reimbursement.
7	Views psychotherapy as almost always benign and useful.	Views psychotherapy as being sometimes useful and sometimes harmful.
8	Sees patient's being in therapy as the most important part of patient's life.	Sees being in the world as more important than being in therapy.

Reproduced with permission from Guilford Publications Inc. From *Theory and Practice of Brief Therapy* by S.H. Budman and A.S. Gurman (1988).

addressed the question of providing psychological therapy efficiently within the NHS.

Short-term counselling is cheaper for funders who, naturally, will not write a blank cheque for time-unlimited services. The existence in the USA of diagnosis-related groups (DRGs) of client problems shows that it is possible to consider in principle, on average, how long certain treatments should take and what they may cost. Counsellors object to such moves partly in defence of their clients' needs but also, probably, because they are unused to being economically and clinically accountable. It has been argued that much counselling and psychotherapy is based on guesswork and well-intentioned but vague processes (see Feltham, 1995), but now counsellors are having to think hard about whether they can deliver reasonably defined results within time constraints. There is also a social-ethical issue involved here: the more efficient and time-conscious counsellors can be (particularly within the NHS), the more therapeutic time is made available for others who otherwise languish on waiting lists. This is in turn linked with the clinical and economic concern about the optimal time for clients to receive counselling so as to prevent subsequent psychological or psychosomatic illness.

What rapidly becomes apparent for private practitioners is that time-limited counselling does not pay, or at least it presents problems because it brings constant turnover of business and probable gaps in one's schedule. As Budman and Gurman put it (see Table 2.1), the long-term therapist is unconsciously aware of the fiscal inconvenience of short-term work. This is obviously not a good reason for clients to regard long-term therapy as the norm.

Clinical efficiency
Clinical efficiency is, of course, related to economics but the emphasis is on the best use of time to help clients alleviate what they want alleviated. Clinical orientations which traditionally show little concern for treatment of choice usually proceed to explore clients' concerns in a leisurely manner in the belief that underlying dynamics will eventually be identified and lead to some degree of resolution. Approaches like multimodal therapy set out to assess and address as directly as possible each client's real needs and how these may be met with systematically eclectic efficiency. Lazarus's (1989) argument is that global theories and their associated practices inefficiently treat every client as if he or she must fit the grand theory, rather than first addressing the obvious and attempting the most likely remedy. Gratuitous history-taking may be an error here, also using excessively non-directive methods to treat post-traumatic stress, for example, when arguably more efficient methods such as eye movement desensitisation are available, and so on.

If we are to take seriously the research of Howard et al. (1986) on the dose-effect curve, which argues that the most significant amount of change across a client population occurs early on in therapy (62 per cent of clients have been helped within 13 sessions). Although this is not conclusive evidence of anything, it does force us to ask uncomfortable questions about the time we take to do counselling and therapy. Combined with clients' views on preferred length of therapy and mean attendance rates (often put at around six sessions), the evidence is that we have not paid sufficient attention to what we do, and what more we can do, within the first few sessions.

Consider too the effect of deadlines of people. Many find a firm temporal structure reassuring (Mohamed and Smith, 1996; Macnab, 1993) and seem less likely to drop out when contained by a time constraint (Sledge et al., 1990). Deadlines frequently have the effect of concentrating the mind. It may be that firm but flexibly contracted deadlines offer a good way forward for clinical practice (Elton Wilson, 1996).

Minimal waste and damage
One of the most serious criticisms of traditional, long-term, relationship-based therapy is that dependency is created, presenting problems are either unaddressed or left unresolved, and clients are sometimes emotionally and financially worse off at the end of it than before (Carlson, 1995). If there is any truth in these remarks (and there obviously is for a number of clients), then what harm is done will be logically reduced in short-term therapy or counselling. This is not the strongest argument in favour of time-limited work but it is a significant one. It could be said that short-term counselling is generally safer than long-term and that it is always more economical for clients. If you pay as a private client, specifically time-limited counselling would give you the chance to calculate how much you will spend (e.g. 10 sessions at £30 will be exactly £300), whereas the cost of open-ended therapy is obviously indeterminate and usually will, in fact, run into thousands of pounds. Even if you are unhappy with the results of your time-limited counselling, you would have lost a lot less than if you had spent thousands of pounds on therapy with poor results.

Striano (1988) cites many cases of psychotherapy clients she calls therapy addicts, who have endured years of unproductive therapy. Due to their own dependency, wish to please their therapists, inability to terminate in the face of their therapists' protestations or manipulation, these people have often forfeited large sums of money, failed to get better and, in many cases, have deteriorated. One of the challenges of time-limited therapy is that it places an onus of accountability on therapists and counsellors. Time-limited work does not rule out extendable contracts but does keep temporal reality in focus. In the case of deterioration, a policy of regular reviews would help to prevent people from remaining in iatrogenic therapy.

Client preferences

Most clinical practitioners must have observed that many clients, of their own volition, attend relatively very few sessions of therapy. Having worked in a wide variety of counselling agencies, including those where no time limits are imposed, I have seen that there is often an average take-up of around three or four sessions for each client. In one agency offering an initial contract of up to six sessions, the mean number actually used is 3.5–3.75 (Goss, 1995). Many clients attend therapy only once and choose not to return, not necessarily due to dissatisfaction or defensiveness (as is often assumed) but because they had not expected to attend longer and do not feel a need to (Talmon, 1990). According to one source, between 20 per cent and 55 per cent of clients attend therapy on only one occasion (Cooper, 1995). Agency managers working within time-limited services have often observed that many clients who have six or eight sessions available to them choose to attend only once or twice.

By contrast, counsellors and therapists have generally experienced lengthy or ongoing therapy themselves as part of their own training, have often been taught not to accept superficial change but to probe for deep dynamics, and enjoy lengthy psychological mining ventures. It has taken a long time for them to come to terms with the voice and behaviour of the consumer. Pekarik and Finney-Owen (1987) found that therapists' estimates of how much therapy their clients needed exceeded the clients' own estimates by a factor of three to one. Perhaps people typically wish to seek therapy only when something hurts and they wish to engage in it only as long as it feels necessary – for the time being. The once and for all psychological upheaval and reconstruction model of the therapists is not shared by most consumers, and Cummings and Sayama (1995) may have got it right when they dwell on the practice of intermittent therapy. This is not to say that *some* clients do not prefer lengthy, ongoing therapy, but these are probably in a minority and many of them tend to be directly involved in the culture and profession of psychotherapy and personal growth. We

need to consider, within both our training and practice as counsellors and therapists, to what extent we really listen to what
clients say, as opposed to preferring and delivering what suits us.
Since practitioners are mostly middle class, for example, they
need to consider the hidden implications of the class gap between
themselves and many of their clients.

All counselling and therapy contains temporal assumptions

A powerful argument is that all therapy is in fact limited in, and
organised around, time and that the current movement towards
explicit recognition of this fact has simply forced us to confront it.
As I have pointed out, psychoanalytic sessions are traditionally 50-
minutes long. Why? There is no evidence that this length of time
suits clients, or that daily sessions of this length lead to better
outcomes. Indeed, the opposite is probably true – that clients are
diverse in their needs and what would suit them best is that each
of their needs is accommodated on an individual basis. To some
extent this has been recognised by those humanistic therapists
who offer longer sessions (one and a half, two hours, half or
whole days, or even marathon group sessions). Writing on the
taboo against long individual sessions (Older, 1977) suggests that
traditional ('Your time is up') therapy has had its own, often
countertherapeutic reasons for imposing strict sessional time
limits. 'I *know* that I have gone further and have been of more use
to a patient in four intensive hours at night than in forty separate
hours at three o'clock on Tuesday afternoons', Older insists (1977:
202).

The idea that sessions are usually or have to be 50 minutes or
an hour in length may itself be a myth. French psychoanalyst
Lacan sometimes dramatically shortened the traditional therapy
hour. Milton Erickson sometimes spent only minutes with certain
clients, or he would see someone for several hours without a
break (Budman and Gurman, 1988: 283). Albert Ellis, founder of
rational emotive behaviour therapy, prefers half-hour sessions.
Forty or forty-five minute sessions are not uncommon. Wilson
(1981) argues that therapists are traditionally ruled by the arbitrary
50-minute session, which leads often to uncreative and unrespon-
sive therapy. Citing research on the flexible use of time in
behaviour therapy, he suggests that two-hour sessions of *in vivo*
exposure can be much more effective than four separate half-hour

sessions. Sex therapy, in certain instances, may be more effective in 'massed' (concentrated) time spans than in 'distributed' sessions. Wilson also comments that intensive time in therapy in the beginning followed by a pattern of less frequent sessions may be optimal.

Castelnuovo-Tedesco (1986), also questioning the sacred 50-minute session, argued that general practitioners could offer beneficial supportive psychotherapy in 20-minute sessions over a typical time span of 10 weeks. Perry (1989) has argued that in relation to borderline clients careful thought should always be given to optimal session length and frequency of sessions, and negotiation may be called for. Perry also notes that for certain clients 20 minutes is probably optimal. Zirkle (1961) argued that for many hospitalised schizophrenic patients, scheduled daily contacts of five minutes' duration were better received than weekly scheduled sessions of 25 minutes. I have sometimes advised supervisees that some of their clients may be better served by twice weekly sessions of 30 minutes rather than once weekly hour-long sessions. Such an arrangement appears to meet the needs of both (particularly distressed, confused or unsupported) clients and under-resourced agencies.

Malan (1976) points out that any set number of sessions may be distributed over different periods of time. He maintains that a firm ending date is more important than the precise number of sessions. According to Malan, such arrangements are usually more beneficial than harmful. But even Malan stops short of recommending absolutely non-negotiable time limits in every case, as Mann (1973) does. Interestingly, Malan (1976: 40) states that 'there is no special magic in any particular number of sessions', providing that clients know exactly what is on offer. It may be useful for readers to consider this disclaimer about an optimal number of sessions because I have repeatedly encountered questions which imply that perhaps there should or must be a magic or most effective number.

Some counsellors endorse the practice of scheduling a number of sample sessions with every new client. For example, it may be agreed that four or six meetings be held, at the end of which time both parties will decide how well they think they can work together, and after that counselling becomes open-ended. Others prefer to hold regular reviews after every, say, six or ten sessions. Macnab (1993) is one of few practitioners who purposefully organises therapy around six-session modules, each aiming to address particular problem areas. Certainly some counselling agencies have decided on renewable contracts of six sessions at a time, which often seems to be appreciated by clients, giving as it does both structure and flexibility (Goss, 1995). Elton Wilson (1996) advocates a contractual model of time-conscious therapy which may offer one to three holding sessions, four to six sessions based on a 'mini-commitment', 10 to 13 sessions of time-focused therapy, and 'time-extended' and 'time-expanded' therapeutic contracts of up to four to five years, with periods of notice for termination clearly contracted. It is a quite common practice for therapists to contract with clients that they will attend a certain number of sessions, say four, after they have decided to terminate therapy, in order to work through any issues relating to ending. In all these ways, the importance of time (not always the importance the *client* attaches to time!) is demonstrated.

Presence and the eternal now

The time boundary in time-limited therapy is usually presented as a constraining factor. Long-term or at least open-ended therapy has been the norm for years and it now seems that something is being conceded. Brief therapists have argued that such traditional therapy might be considered protracted therapy, with brief therapy coming to be regarded as the norm. Another way of looking at time in therapy is to suggest that therapy is only truly therapeutic when time is transcended. This does not mean psychoanalytic timelessness, however.

I have argued elsewhere that certain charismatic and fortuitous encounters must be considered in any discussion of psychotherapy and counselling (Feltham, 1995). Beyond our habitual, fallible efforts to help others or to extricate ourselves from suffering, there are moments of freedom. Within phenomena such as grace, serendipity, the I–Thou meeting, transcendence or the eternal now, some of us sometimes touch a realm beyond problems – an egoless state of being, a perspective from which all habitual human problems evaporate. Some have discussed this as arising out of heightened presence in the therapy session. Others have referred to the moment of responsibility, when the client suddenly sees clearly that he or she is not chained to the past or doomed to a particular future. Everyday human problems constitute the

baggage we all seem to carry around with us, whether in the form
of phobias, anxieties, obsessions, depression, or general
dissatisfaction. In counselling sessions two human beings meet
who are both subject to everyday human problems, the hope
being that one who is somewhat freer will help the other to be
somewhat freer. It is thought that this helping process takes time
(a short time or a long time).

It is possible, however, to consider the therapy hour as exactly
the same eternal now as the rest of life. We haul our problems
around with us outside therapy and we pick over them inside
therapy. The therapist or counsellor tends to bring his or her
habitual strategies, theories and personality to each session and –
however closely the client is tracked, attended and reacted to –
there is usually a therapeutic agenda (the counsellor's) meeting a
problematic self-concept (the client's). The possibility that both
might simultaneously meet a new, discontinuous kind of energy
or presence – the healing of the eternal now – is usually
overlooked. Or it may be that heightened presence sometimes
acts alongside clinical manoeuvres, giving the impression that
therapeutic techniques or therapist-provided conditions have
achieved change. The asocial character of the therapy session
(freedom to speak and emote uninhibitedly, to experiment, to re-
invent oneself, to receive another's undivided attention, and so
on) facilitates contact, perhaps, with a quality of time or freedom
from time which is in itself curative. In this state of being, our
everyday preoccupations and chronic distress are momentarily
washed away. For the most part, our traumas and losses belong to
the past and our fears, too, are based on the past. In the actual
present, there are very few real problems for those of us who are
not starving or in physical pain.

I believe that glimpses of the eternal now, this problem-
transcending state of consciousness, are had by most people.
Instances of such breakthroughs in counselling are traceable in
the ideas of introducing novelty into therapy (Cummings, 1990a;
Cade and O'Hanlon, 1993); in finding exceptions to problem
behaviour and entertaining the miracle question (de Shazer,
1991); in experiencing the transpersonal relationship (Clarkson,
1995); and in the ideas of immediacy and the here and now in
Gestalt and psychodynamic counselling. In the acknowledgement
that there are moments of great presence in therapy, as well as
moments of honestly not knowing, there are hints at a real and

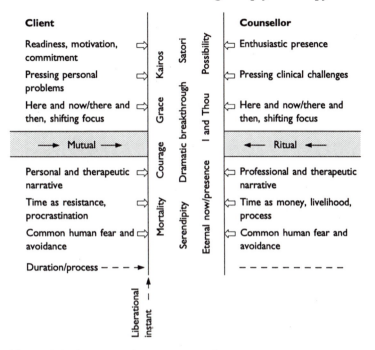

Figure 2.1 *Duration and instant in counselling*

potent, time and problem-transcending realm (Krishnamurti and Bohm, 1985). Brazier (1995: 71) suggests that 'helping the client to develop [Zen] mindfulness of their own account . . . can speed therapy up enormously, since it gives the client the reins.' Carlson (1995) presents the view that a commitment to living in the here and now circumvents the need for therapy. It is not true to say that the only concern of time-limited counsellors is to save time and money: the meaning, analysis and therapeutic power of time and its transcendence is also at the heart of the question of time-limited counselling (Slife, 1993). Appendix 1 demonstrates an argument somewhat along these lines. This report, not easily found elsewhere, is included here because it may be of special interest to readers wishing to explore non-economic (philosophical or mystical) arguments against temporal process in therapy; see also Krishnamurti and Bohm (1985). Figure 2.1 shows something of the relationship that exists between therapeutic *duration* and liberational *instant* (Whitrow, 1988).

3

Kinds and Models of Short-Term and Time-Limited Counselling and Psychotherapy

Estimates vary as to how many current models of counselling or therapy exist, but the figure is probably around 300 or 400. If each of these models could be offered on a short-term, time-limited basis, then of course the number of time-limited models would be around 300 or 400 too. (For a sample of very different short-term approaches, see Marteau, 1986; Zeig and Gilligan, 1990; Ryle, 1990; Gersie, 1996; Dryden, 1995; and Molnos, 1995.) But many models, particularly within the depth psychology camp, do not naturally lend themselves to short-term treatment. Even designated short-term psychoanalytic therapy has been recorded as taking up to 40 sessions (Malan, 1963). Person-centred counselling too, because of its emphasis on placing decision-making power in the hands of the client, does not adapt easily to time-limited work, in spite of recorded instances of some time-limited experiments and successes (Rogers and Dymond, 1954; Thorne, 1994). Broadly speaking, humanistic and psychoanalytic models of counselling are likely to be more resistant than others to the enforced limits of time and economic arguments to support these. (An exception lies in those transpersonal, consciousness-raising groups which attempt to bring about radically altered states of consciousness in a short time.) The cognitive–behavioural and eclectic models are likely to lend themselves more naturally to short-term work than others.

It is useful for practitioners of time-limited counselling or therapy to have an overview of approaches in this field, in part so that they have a background knowledge of approaches before them but also because a degree of eclecticism is arguably necessary (Garfield, 1995; Pollin, 1995). These approaches can be roughly divided into three types of model.

1 Models adapted or designed to be relatively brief, although not necessarily having a pre-set time limit (e.g. the short-term dynamic therapy of Malan, Davanloo and others; Budman and Gurman's interpersonal-developmental-existential (IDE) approach).
2 Models which naturally lend themselves to brief or time-sensitive work (e.g. behaviour therapy, cognitive therapy, rational emotive behaviour therapy, multimodal therapy, reality therapy, Egan's three-stage approach, solution-focused brief therapy, neuro-linguistic programming).
3 Models which are purposefully designed to be short-term and time-limited (e.g. Mann's 12 session model, cognitive analytic therapy, single-session therapy, the two-plus-one model, contextual modular therapy).

Certain approaches, such as transactional analysis, experiential psychotherapy, dramatherapy and focused expressive psychotherapy can be adapted contractually to address either short-term, focused agendas or more long-term personal growth work (see also Elton Wilson, 1996). Here, I outline very briefly a selection of relevant approaches, with some references given for readers who wish to investigate them in greater depth. Fuller accounts of comparative models can be found in Budman (1981), Wells and Gianetti (1990) and Budman et al. (1992).

Short-term dynamic therapy

Ironically, it is the tradition that most obviously espouses long-term psychotherapy which has also generated some of the earliest bids for meaningful short-term therapy. From many of Freud's early brief cases to Ferenczi's active therapy, Rank's will therapy, Skekel's focused therapy, Alexander and French's focus on the corrective emotional experience, the psychoanalytic tradition has also spawned Sifneos's anxiety-provoking therapy, Mann's time-limited psychotherapy, Balint's focal psychotherapy, Malan's brief psychotherapy, Davanloo's intensive short-term dynamic psychotherapy and Wolberg's eclectic short-term psychotherapy (Flegenheimer, 1982; Molnos, 1995). Obviously there are many differences between these approaches but I intend here to dwell more on the commonalities.

Brief psychodynamic approaches are all likely to insist on the importance of boundaries. These boundaries may include time, place, security, confidentiality, therapist non-disclosure, certain conduct and so on (Molnos, 1995). These are not sacrificed to the demands of time-limited work. However, Molnos makes the interesting point that consulting rooms should be well lit, clients should be seated face to face and the environment should *discourage* the typical psychoanalytic sense of timelessness and cosy self-reflection. Brief dynamic psychotherapy (I use the terms dynamic, psychodynamic, therapy, psychotherapy and counselling fairly interchangeably in this context) uses or makes reference to transference, countertransference, defence mechanisms and the relationship between the client's personal past, present and therapeutic relationship in the same way as longer-term versions. The chief difference is in the attitude to time.

As Molnos puts it, 'transference needs no time' (1995: 47). In other words, transference is evident from the first contact in the many nuances of the client's behaviour. Therapists like Davanloo waste no time in identifying early instances of transference (for example, pointing out to the client her passive–aggressive stance towards him) but does this in the context of assessment (trial therapy refers to early efforts to test out the client's ability to work in this intensive way) and non-judgemental confrontation of defences. Critics who have scorned such approaches for their aggressive style have often failed to note that the therapist seeks to convey acceptance of the person and a therapeutic alliance with them against their self-sabotaging strategies. It is interesting to consider Molnos's (1995) view that many analytic or dynamic therapists are themselves guilty of manifesting temporal resistance. In other words, as practitioners they are often defensively wedded to long-term, protracted and perhaps avoidant ways of working.

Psychodynamic counsellors wishing to engage in short-term, time-limited counselling or therapy need particularly to reckon with their own possible resistances. Malan (1963) discussed 12 lengthening factors in (dynamic) therapy and Molnos (1995) has extended these to 19. They include the problems of unconscious resistance itself, working-through, dependency, passivity, sense of timelessness, therapeutic perfectionism, and a 'preoccupation with ever deeper and earlier experiences' (Malan, 1963: 9). Malan also notes that waning enthusiasm on the part of experienced therapists may also protract therapy. In addition, Molnos stresses the problems of the 'lure of timelessness', free association, over-determination (wanting to get at all possible root causes and related factors) and transference neurosis. Furthermore, she adds, there is social pressure within psychoanalytic circles to observe conventions of lengthy therapy, and that private practice and short-term therapy do not mix very happily! (1995: 16–17).

What do brief dynamic psychotherapists or counsellors actually do? Obviously they reduce the lengthening factors mentioned above. Therapeutic perfectionism, for example, simply has to be dispensed with when working briefly, and a level of 'good enough' knowledge of the client's past and key conflicts must similarly be accepted. What is needed are a modest number of focal conflicts upon which to work. These may best relate to problems of recent onset in the client's life. Molnos (1995) suggests that loss, abandonment, rage and problem solving are appropriate foci and that exploration of the unconscious should give way to exploration of the problem pattern.

The triangle of insight (between the client's past and present relationships and their relationship with the therapist) is utilised as rapidly as possible. A high level of challenge may be made but in such a way, in very brief contracts, that ego strength is increased or maintained; in longer-term work (up to 40 sessions) more defence-dismantling work can be engaged in. Clues to just how much challenge as opposed to supportive interpretation can be managed are gained from early trial therapy – testing out the client's resilience, commitment, readiness and insight. The therapist is likely to be active from the outset, especially when counselling may be very brief indeed (Coren, 1996). Attention to the triangle of defences, anxiety (as defences are threatened) and access to real feelings is advisable. Keeping the time frame in mind and working directly with feelings about being short-changed or about loss are useful strategies.

The time-limited psychodynamic counsellor practises with many of the same procedures as in long-term work, but much more intensively and in relation to a realistic cluster of foci. Brief dynamic therapists vary in their views on assessment and suitability, on length of therapy and whether an ending date should be fixed. (Mann is one of the very few committed to a fixed time and to using time itself as a central psychodynamic focus.) Most carefully observe developmental factors expressed unconsciously by the client. Readers especially interested in developing their time-limited counselling competency should consult Malan (1963, 1976), Mann (1973), Davanloo (1990), Molnos (1995) and, for an overview, Flegenheimer (1982).

Rational emotive behaviour therapy

Albert Ellis began creating rational emotive behaviour therapy (REBT) in New York the 1950s. Trained as a psychoanalyst, he was unhappy about the time traditional analysis took and the inconclusive results achieved. He became more interested in how people perpetuate their problems than in how these might have arisen in the first place. According to Ellis, insight, interpretation and all the therapeutic talk in the world is insufficient to overthrow deeply ingrained irrational thinking, and its emotional and behavioural consequences. We constantly re-indoctrinate ourselves with various irrational beliefs. We believe, for example, that the world should be the way we want it to be, it should be comfortable and accommodating; and when it is not we are bound to be very upset, frustrated, depressed and so on. We typically attribute our feelings to events around us (past, present or future), failing to recognise that it is not these events themselves but our interpretations of them that upset us. If we learn rationally to accept frustration and disappointment and to work at changing what it is possible to change with hard work, we will be healthier. Rather than telling ourselves how catastrophic adversity is, if we put adversity into proportion we are more likely to handle it well and overcome it sooner. REBT is, then, a form of stoical therapy, a programme of personal re-education which is not dependent on unearthing the idiosyncratic causes of each client's concerns.

Clinically, REBT relies on finding focal concerns, on analysing the ways in which clients convince themselves that events are intrinsically disturbing and helping them to test out the rationality or otherwise of their beliefs. What is the client telling himself about the forthcoming event at which he has to give a speech? That everybody will be looking intently at him, ready for him to make the slightest error, which will be noted; that people will laugh at him, that he will feel dreadful, never live it down, and so on. He is winding himself up to feel bad, to perform badly and to judge himself harshly for a long time to come. The therapist will help him to see that his speech may go well or well enough, instead of disastrously; that even if he performs poorly he will probably not be judged harshly, that people probably will not laugh but be sympathetic, and so on. Even if it goes badly, it will soon be forgotten by everyone. Furthermore, what if it does go badly? What does this prove? That on one forgivable occasion he didn't do so well? He could use the occasion as a learning experience, enabling him to do better next time. Even if in general he is not a good public speaker, is this the end of the world? Probably he is good at many other activities.

REBT has a practical thrust, helping clients to get matters in proportion – putting things into perspective. But it also has a deeper dimension, in which people can be helped radically to challenge their entire philosophical outlook. Instead of being implemented as a crisis remedy, REBT can also be applied to how one lives generally. By examining typical irrational beliefs about the need to have certain things or conditions, or to avoid certain frightening or difficult situations, for example, people can learn to test themselves in many situations and to 'stress-proof' themselves. Ellis has coined the term 'musturbatory' to refer to the habit of insisting that we must have our own way, must be comfortable, must not be rejected, and so on. REBT challenges our shoulds, oughts, musts, awfulising and low frustration tolerance.

Ellis is happy to use forcefulness in therapy, to challenge clients vigorously, directively to set them homework assignments which may confront them with their worst fears. In the shame-attacking exercise for which REBT is famous, you might be asked to do something apparently outrageous or exhibitionistic, thereby inviting people to look at you and laugh at you, perhaps to think you stupid, for example. If you dread humiliation, by deliberately exposing yourself to something you imagine will be humiliating, you can meet it on your terms, give yourself the opportunity to monitor your thoughts and your reactions and to discuss these later with your therapist. Techniques (disputing, imagery, shame-attacking exercises, bibliotherapy, etc.) are used eclectically in the service of challenging irrational beliefs and discovering more productive rational ones.

Ellis himself conducts 30-minute sessions out of preference for the efficient use of time. He is concerned to help people not merely to feel better temporarily but to get better and stay better. He argues that REBT, which is usually conducted on a short-term basis (often with follow-up or booster sessions) achieves exactly these aims. Dryden (1995) has outlined the use of REBT in an 11-session framework and Ellis (1996) has also written on the application of REBT in the context of brief therapy.

If you are opposed to methods like REBT on the grounds that they appear to ignore or minimise the past, fail to observe unconscious processes, play down the therapeutic relationship and address only presenting concerns, consider at least the possibility that for certain clients this may be the approach of choice. Consider, too, the possibility of challenging yourself with some REBT homework assignments in order to hone your own skills in time-limited counselling. What do you avoid, postpone or indulge in too much? Are there aspects of your life that could benefit from an analysis of your persistent beliefs and chronic avoidances?

Multimodal therapy

Arnold Lazarus, originally trained in psychodynamic and client-centred methods, became one of the foremost behaviour therapists but gradually found that approach too limited and evolved his own, broad spectrum approach, now known as multimodal therapy. Lazarus conceptualised human beings as functioning within at least seven modalities and suggested that behaviour is only one of these. Using the acronym BASIC ID, Lazarus suggests that we can be understood in terms of:

- behaviour (what we do or avoid that characterises us or causes us problems);
- affect (how and what we typically feel and express, such as anger, sadness, anxiety, fear, etc.);
- sensation (typical bodily sensations or aesthetic sensitivities

such as muscle tension, blushing, palpitations, gastro-intestinal mobility, preference for or avoidance of certain sights, tastes, etc.);

- imagery (typical good or bad experiences of or preferences for certain images, including imaginal metaphors, flashbacks, dreams, nightmares, etc.);
- cognition (thinking patterns, including irrational and negative thinking, problem-solving or intellectualisation);
- interpersonal (family, partner, colleagues, culture, and how these help or hinder personal effectiveness and happiness);
- drugs/biology (medication, substance abuse, nutritional habits, exercise and lifestyle factors, etc.).

The great strength of multimodal therapy is that it offers the means for comprehensively assessing with clients their concerns and getting a handle on them promptly. The BASIC ID can be used (but should not be used slavishly) at intake to determine the most pressing concerns and the best methods of addressing them. Lazarus is in favour of identifying what the client wants or needs to work on and what is likely to be the most effective therapeutic agent. For example, if the client is suffering from situational panic attacks, in general the most likely remedy will be some form of behavioural desensitisation approach perhaps, or relaxation training. However, if assessment indicates that the client is primarily a thinker, therapy may be tailored to begin with more cognitive techniques. Multimodal assessment is offered as a guide to orientate the therapeutic process. It is systematically eclectic (not theoretically integrative), and aims to relieve suffering and correct faulty patterns of behaviour, according to clients' unique needs. Lazarus is pragmatic enough to recognise a need to adapt to the client's personality and preferred way of working. He is prepared to utilise techniques from diverse therapeutic approaches, including those he does not believe in theoretically.

Multimodal therapy lends itself to being brief because it is pragmatic and focused. As Lazarus and Fay (1990: 36) put it:

> Good therapy is precise. A session should contain no unnecessary psychological tests, no protracted or redundant methods, no needless techniques, no prolonged silences, and as little dilatory rhetoric as possible. This requires not that the therapist gloss over important details, nor that he or she forgo thoroughness for the sake of brevity, but that every intervention tell.

A good way of sampling multimodal therapy is to watch the well-known training video, featuring the client Kathy, in which Lazarus covers a lot of ground in a very short time in one session. See also Palmer and Dryden (1995).

Brief solution-focused therapy

Stemming from family therapy and inspired by figures like Gregory Bateson, Milton Erickson and Jay Haley, this approach – often known simply as brief therapy – is characterised by an emphasis on solutions rather than psychopathology. We can readily observe that people make attempts at solving their problems that often fail; similarly, therapists rooted in particular traditions may have limited successes because they repeatedly use the same methods. Solution-focused brief therapists are inclined to 'try something different' (de Shazer, 1991).

People in difficulty are doing the best they can but often inadvertently dig deeper holes for themselves. We view things through our habitual constructs and act according to them. Many of our problems derive from simple habits which become complex and unhelpful over time, and we remain inclined to rely on familiar response patterns – however painful or counterproductive these become. We may become enmeshed in systems of self-fulfilling prophecy and 'hardening of the categories' (O'Hanlon, 1990). For all of us, it is all too easy to confuse our fixed conceptual frameworks with inevitably shifting realities.

The practice of brief therapy is founded on what is observable rather than on putative causes. The therapist must be alert to the client's behaviour on beginning therapy: does it signify desire for actual change or not? What is the person getting and not getting out of their behaviour? When do their typical problems occur and not occur? What does the problem behaviour look like in action? Around which people do the problems occur? Brief therapists ask for exceptions to the problem occurring, dislodging the belief that the client is, for example, *always* depressed. (This is similar to cognitive therapy procedures.) How do clients manifest their problems within the session? (Without concepts of transference, brief therapists still observe and work with what clients actually do in sessions, including what they do in relation to the therapist.) Questions are asked about clients' existing explanations for their own problems and attempted solutions.

Crucially, clients are asked to envisage and describe what the solution to their problems would look like, and therefore what will signal success in therapy (Cade and O'Hanlon, 1993). This approach is strongly future-focused and only 'skeleton keys' are sought, in contrast to the over-deterministic tendencies of many long-term therapists.

Clients may be asked to try out new behaviours as experiments. They will certainly be challenged with a new, novel and even paradoxical reframing of their perspectives on their problems. Since people tend to practise a 'more of the same' approach to life's difficulties, both clients and counsellors can easily become stuck in their particular mind-sets. Clients may be asked in brief therapy to identify exceptions to their habitual misery – times when it does not occur – or reasons why it is not worse than it is. One of the central catalytic interventions in this approach is the so-called miracle question. By asking a client to imagine that a miracle occurs that night, solving their problem, they are then led on to describe how it would look – how they and others would notice the changes – in detail. This concentration on future possibilities liberates the problem-solving capacities we probably all have and challenges the fatalism that is implicit in most clients' problem-construal. Solution-focused brief therapists aim to become highly skilled, pragmatic clinicians, ready to use stories, metaphors, reinforcement of existing coping skills, paradoxical interventions and other aids to change. O'Hanlon (1990) summarises the work of this approach as simply changing the viewing and changing the doing (this applies to counsellors as well as to clients!).

This form of brief therapy is not deliberately or contractually time-limited as such. However, practitioners aim to do their work in as few sessions as possible and regard each session as, potentially, the last. The average number of sessions is under five, 95 per cent of cases involve under 10 sessions, and sessions are sometimes weeks or months apart. Interestingly, solution-focused therapists attribute the brevity of their therapy to locating expertise in the client, which means that therapists cannot themselves know or determine how long it should take (Iveson, personal communication, 1996). This is to turn the logic of many psychodynamic and person-centred counsellors – that if left to the client the therapy will probably be long-term – on its head.

Cognitive analytic therapy

Cognitive analytic therapy (known commonly as CAT) is a time-limited form of psychotherapy, created originally by Anthony Ryle from elements of personal construct therapy (which Ryle regards as a basically cognitive approach) and object relations theory. CAT seeks to help clients understand their self-defeating behaviour and core neurotic problems by means of adapted repertory grid techniques (borrowed from personal construct therapy). Ryle has referred to typical self-defeating behaviour patterns as dilemmas, traps and snags and new clients are given a psychotherapy file which steers them through a questionnaire designed to elicit these patterns (see Appendix 2). The procedural sequence model was devised as a way of helping clients to describe and understand how they repeatedly put their dysfunctional interpretative patterns into action. 'Self-maintaining vicious circles' is one of the terms used by Ryle to describe how people typically repeat distressing or troublesome behaviour.

CAT is an integrative model of therapy recognising the value of certain psychodynamic explanations for problematic behaviour, along with the value of making thought patterns overt and behaviour controllable. Accurate description and non-collusion are key elements of CAT, as is the encouragement of active participation by the client in understanding his or her behaviour and attempting to change it. Ryle developed CAT, conscious of NHS waiting lists and the unrealistically long treatment periods characterising psychoanalytic therapies. Much of the clinical work in CAT has been confined to 16 sessions in a truly time-limited model. Ample use of questionnaires, diagrams, homework assignments and other written material is made in CAT. These tools both encourage clients to collaborate in understanding their behaviour and provide a structure from which to work efficiently. To some extent, the power of CAT seems to rest on the containment offered by the structure of its explanatory models. These models offer, to some degree, 'takeaway therapy' tools with which clients may continue to work. It is acknowledged that CAT is often useful as a first therapy, as a constructive aid in self-harming crises and as a good enough therapy for people otherwise deprived of the means of getting some purchase on their self-defeating patterns. The goodbye letter often written by both client and therapist at the end of the 16 weeks is a means of acknowledging the imperfection of the therapy, the valuable ground covered and the map created for traversing future personal growth.

CAT is a fast-growing therapy that has gained considerable respect within the NHS and in other settings, both in Britain and in other countries. It has been closely and responsibly researched for several years and shows promise of delivering sustained positive results and of becoming a significant part of NHS psychological provision (Ryle, 1995) and in voluntary organisations (Mohamed and Smith, 1996).

Since CAT is itself an integrative model of short-term therapy with clearly defined clinical procedures, it is reasonable to ask whether it can be adapted or used eclectically alongside other approaches. Ryle does not deny that CAT resembles, for example, the approach of Paul Wachtel known as cyclical psychodynamics (Gold and Wachtel, 1993). To some extent CAT seems to resemble transactional analysis, with its partly psychoanalytic roots and its mission to simplify therapeutic language and to give clients tools for change. It is acknowledged that various techniques (transference interpretation and Gestalt role plays, for example) may be used within CAT. Is it possible to borrow aspects of CAT itself in a generic or personal model of time-limited counselling, without adopting CAT wholesale? Ryle himself sees no objection to this (personal communication, 1995).

Critics of CAT have objected to the use of up to four sessions for assessment, and its reliance on paper assessments, diagrams, and so on. Undoubtedly much of the success of CAT stems from its assessment procedure and its apparent rendering of the chaos and complexity of clients' lives into manageable core issues and goals to be worked upon.

Brief intermittent psychotherapy throughout the life cycle

The traditional model of once-and-for-all therapy lasting perhaps two or three years (or more), that restructures the personality and clears up many or most problems, has been challenged. It does not actually work that way, say critics, it is not an efficient use of time, and, however healthy and happy we may be at one time in our lives, we are always vulnerable to accidents, losses and shocks. Brief intermittent therapy throughout the life cycle – sometimes referred to as episodic or serial short-term therapy –

has been posited as more realistic on many grounds. Many have made contributions to this way of thinking but Nick Cummings is one of its primary advocates (Cummings, 1990b; Cummings and Sayama, 1995).

In Cummings's view we commonly repeat early distress patterns and early attempted solutions, however counterproductive these are. We all encounter developmental crises associated with starting school, becoming adults, making partnerships, and experiencing separations, ageing and death. At various points in our lives we are likely to repeat old distress patterns, somewhat idiosyncratic to ourselves perhaps but usually identifiable. Since anxiety is an inescapable part of living, there can be no cure for it. Since clients develop, change, and find their own solutions before and after therapy, it is not sensible to think in terms of 'being in therapy'. Rather, people need access to (preferably consistent) professional helping figures across their life span. Cummings is in favour of the psychological equivalent of the medical GP – someone with experience, expertise and familiarity with the client and his or her development and family, who can be consulted as and when necessary.

Brief intermittent psychotherapy is targeted on clients' actual problems and therefore is not rooted in grand, monolithic theoretical traditions. The therapist addresses the crisis or developmental issue presented at any one time, the next time another issue or variant is addressed, and so on. Treatment is not, however, simply symptomatic. According to Cummings, 85 per cent of clients opt for this approach and its use cuts down on the overall time needed for therapy, compared with the time it would take to see someone consistently over a period of eight months to a year (Cummings, 1990a). This approach is characterised by immediate, active therapy (no gratuitous history-taking, for example); operational diagnosis (exactly why is the client presenting now?); clear contracting; use of novelty; and regular homework assignments. It appears to be what many clients want, to meet economic arguments and to place the onus on practitioners to become highly skilled strategists instead of therapeutic ideologues.

The two-plus-one model

Like CAT, the two-plus-one model was developed with the reduction of NHS waiting lists at the forefront of its founders' minds. Its name describes its timing – two weekly sessions, followed by another, three months later. This is based on an interpretation of research suggesting that most change occurs very early on in therapy (Howard et al., 1986) and that a third of clients are probably served successfully by very brief therapy. The longer therapy continues, the more the gains are in the area of 'fine-tuning' rather than 'high impact' (Dryden, 1992: 23). The benefits of this model, were it to be offered widely, are that it can obviously reach a larger number of people than traditional long-term models and can be delivered without a long waiting period.

Having been developed and tested within a research environment, the two-plus-one model takes into account the process of change across time rather than aiming for single session success. The first two sessions are designed to produce a strong impact – giving clients a rationale, a period in which to engage in self-change and a holding structure. The period of three months that follows allows for self-change or self-reflection. The model does not claim to help everyone or to be a panacea but is viewed as a realistic means of addressing some clinical needs. It could be safely used as a first therapeutic attempt with most clients; many would be helped sufficiently and those requiring further help might be more efficiently referred. It has been offered responsibly, with preparatory literature being sent out in advance, explaining its reasoning and possible limitations. Both exploratory (psychodynamic–interpersonal) and prescriptive (cognitive–behavioural) orientations have been used within the two-plus-one model, with comparable success (Barkham and Shapiro, 1990). Most of the evaluation of this approach has been carried out with clients with problems of mild to moderate anxiety and stress, but Barkham considers the main exclusion criterion to be severity of distress rather than kind (Dryden, 1992: 22–37). Aveline (1995) has also looked at the distribution of sessions in the NHS and suggested that a four-plus-two model might be advantageous.

Single session therapy

Many counsellors will have observed that a proportion of clients attend for only one session. Perhaps the suspicion has been that this reflects either on the client's resistance or on the counsellor's failure to engage the client successfully. However, it may also be the case that for some clients there has been no expectation that counselling will be an ongoing process (people do not expect to see their GP every week, for example); and for some, one session in which another person listens with undivided attention, non-judgementally and confidentially, is a powerful experience in itself. Talmon (1990) took these factors seriously enough to research them and found that 78 per cent of his clients who had received only one session considered they had significantly improved because of it.

Single session therapy (SST), when it is carried out by design rather than by default, requires pre-session screening and preparation. Clients to be excluded are those who need psychiatric care or who are already wanting long-term therapy. Those with specific problems, those requiring simple reassurance, those with good support systems, who have good previous experiences of overcoming difficulties and who have come to a particular impasse in their lives are all good candidates. But people whose problems are unsolvable can also be helped to accept their situation. Significantly, Talmon argues that many clients actually do not need or will be better off without therapy; Frances and Clarkin (1981) calculated that as many as 35 per cent to 40 per cent of clients who persist with therapy either do not respond or respond negatively. If it is true that about 14 per cent of clients improve even before their first appointment, Talmon may be right to insist that change is under way at the stage of initial phone calls, and that this may be continued and strengthened in a single session.

SST exploits the kind of research and clinical evidence cited above. Armed with the belief that many clients are already changing and will only require one session, Talmon capitalises on factors common to many approaches to short-term therapy. Fostering readiness to change, finding a pivotal focus, identifying clients' strengths and practising solutions are some of the main techniques used. Use of vivid metaphors and hypnotic techniques is also recommended where appropriate. Time is allocated for remaining issues. Simple tasks may be suggested, the client is assured that he or she can return or make contact in future, and follow-up is built in. It is recommended that single session therapists master a wide range of effective skills but approach each session with a sense of 'no history and no future'. The chemistry of a first encounter can be capitalised upon in SST. Sessions may last up to an hour and a half and Talmon recommends that the therapist take a little time out during the session (actually leaving the client briefly) to reflect on major issues and return refreshed and ready to summarise. This can also have dramatic impact. Single session therapists do not pretend that this approach is a panacea or that it is even adequate for some clients. Like the two-plus-one model, SST is presented as a safe bet for many clients and a serious contribution to reducing waiting lists and reaching greater numbers of clients.

Contextual modular therapy

Not widely known in the UK, contextual modular therapy (CMT) was devised by Francis Macnab and colleagues in Australia and is an approach offering six-session modules of therapy (Macnab, 1993). CMT is unusual in attempting to provide planned short-term therapy. Macnab argues that CMT addresses six critical questions:

1 How can early drop-outs from therapy be reduced in number?
2 Can a 'definite plan' for therapy be devised by the practitioner?
3 Can such a plan address specific client problems such as bereavement, post-traumatic stress, social phobias, etc.?
4 Can a truly integrative model of therapy be devised?
5 How can clients be helped to use their strengths, to work collaboratively towards conscious well-being?
6 How can optimal use be made of the first six sessions of therapy; six being a significant number because research repeatedly confirms that clients attend an average of six sessions?

According to Macnab, early application of CMT and research into it suggested that the drop-out rate between first and second sessions fell from 36 per cent to 8 per cent. This and other indicators suggested that a structured, time-limited approach was found by clients to be containing (Sledge et al., 1990). CMT aims to tell clients what to expect, to structure sessions and overall treatment clearly, and to encourage an anti-psychopathological outlook. Both counsellor and client are involved in planning and building coping strategies.

Macnab (1993) claims that concerns as diverse as marital problems, sexual dysfunctions, depression, hypertension, redundancy, jealousy and vindictiveness, simple social phobias, rape and other traumas, bereavement and suicidal tendencies can each be successfully addressed within a planned six-session module. Each session of each module is structured in advance. A first session, for example, might embrace: encounter, empathy, entry; exploring the nature of the problem; coping resources; expectations; previous help; broader issues; establishing priorities and focus; actual therapy; making a contract; a consciously encouraging farewell. Each subsequent session is also structured, with particular emphasis being placed on greetings and farewells that are not regarded as casual. Drawing on research and clinical experience, therapists plan to raise and work on those issues most likely to be present and those strategies most likely to help in each module. In this way, clients are led to expect that therapists understand the nature of the problem, and that reasonably rapid relief and new coping abilities are within reach. Macnab also includes in his approach a realistic module on relapse. Clients are offered some guarantees (that they will be taught certain coping strategies or introduced to significant issues) but are also warned that six sessions may not conclusively solve their problems. Like cognitive analytic therapy, CMT offers active, hopeful, containing and structured time-limited therapy, not a panacea.

This space-limited guide to some of the brief therapies hopefully gives a flavour of the variety of perspectives on short-term work, including some of the skills used. It may be apparent that as a conscientious practitioner you are faced with choosing what to follow up on, what to read next, which training courses to attend, whether to gravitate to an approach that is most like the one you already espouse, and so on. As many writers on time-limited therapy and counselling stress, the primary concern is about helping clients more effectively. Given the diversity of our clients, it seems reasonable to assume that familiarity with a variety of rationales and interventions is more likely to add effectiveness than anxious attachment to any one model.

4

The Appropriateness of Time-Limited Counselling for Different Clients

It is common to hear phrases like, 'Well, of course, brief therapy isn't suitable for clients with anorexia/problems of addiction/problems associated with childhood sexual abuse/personality disorders/severe depression' and so on. Rosen (1990), for example, while liberally regarding brief therapy as having a fairly wide application, states categorically that organic psychoses, schizophrenia, affective psychoses, alcoholism and drug addiction are not suitably treated by brief methods. Other writers have categorically indicated who they believe is unsuitable for brief therapy. Malan (1976) cites an unpublished work by H.P. Hildebrand of the London Clinic of Psycho-analysis in which clients assessed as falling into the following groups might be excluded from brief therapy:

- serious suicide attempts
- drug addiction
- homosexuality
- long-term hospitalisation
- ECT treatment
- chronic alcoholism
- incapacitating chronic obsessional symptoms
- incapacitating chronic phobic symptoms
- gross destructive or self-destructive acting out.

At first sight assertions like these, or some of them, may sound like indisputable clinical wisdom (at least for the time and context in which they were written). When you begin to ask about the severity of alcoholism or acting out, however, along with the client's circumstances, motivation and previous treatment, it is clear that the picture may be more complex, or more open to consideration for brief therapy. Recent accounts of effective treatment of phobias in very few sessions by behaviour therapy or neuro-linguistic programming also throw these diagnostic exclusions into question. Significantly, homosexuality is very unlikely to be commended as suitable for either short-term or long-term treatment today, which is a mark of important changes in views on psychopathology itself.

Cognitive analytic therapy, often of no more than 16 sessions, has been used with many stubborn conditions including personality disorders (Ryle, 1990, 1995). In relation to alcohol problems, Miller et al. (1980) found no significant differences in treatment results when comparing minimal behavioural self-control training (BSCT) with more extensive treatments. Van Bilsen (1996) also commends the use of brief therapy for addictions. Childhood sexual abuse is often thought to be treatable only with long-term therapy, but the work of Herman and Schatzow (1984) and others suggests that this view can be challenged. Hall and Crisp (1987) found positive evidence for lasting gains of brief therapy with anorexic clients. Gersie (1996) suggests that traumatic life events, depression, anxiety, phobias, eating disorders and addictions may all be usefully addressed with brief dramatherapy, and that even certain people coping with myocardial infarction, cancer, asthma and other diseases may be helped.

Chronic, challenging medical conditions (including multiple sclerosis, lupus, heart disease, cancer and kidney disease) are addressed within 10 or fewer structured sessions by the medical crisis counselling model of Pollin (1995). Hunter (1994) commends time-limited counselling in the context of obstetrics and gynaecology. Pugh (1992) indicates that children facing grief and bereavement may often be helped significantly by very brief interventions. Snow (1996) argues that psychosis can also be worked with using brief dramatherapy. Victims of rape, too, can be helped with brief (cognitive) therapy, according to Resick and Mechanic (1995). Indeed a search of the literature reveals that very few conditions escape the attention of brief and time-limited

Table 4.1 *Differential time span considerations*

Time	Issue	References
1 session	Depression, anxiety, obesity, divorce, etc.	Talmon, 1990
	Phobias	Marks, 1989; Andreas and Andreas, 1992
	Post-traumatic stress	McCann, 1992
	Self-harming	Cowmeadow, 1995
	Panic attacks	Palmer and Dryden, 1995
1–3 sessions	Mild depression	Barkham and Shapiro, 1990
1–6 sessions	Work stress	Goss, 1995
6 sessions	Interpersonal difficulties	Maple, 1985
	Crisis intervention	Freeman, 1968
	Social phobias	Macnab, 1993
6–12 sessions	Marital problems	Freeman, 1990; Macnab, 1993
9 sessions	Failing eyesight	Grant et al., 1993
10 sessions	Medical crises	Pollin, 1995
11 sessions	Time management, assertiveness, low self-esteem	Dryden, 1995
12–16 sessions	Core personality conflicts	Mann, 1973; Ryle, 1990
	Anorexia nervosa	Hall and Crisp, 1987
16 sessions	Personality disorders	Ryle, 1990

The time spans given above offer some indication of the kinds of client concerns that have reportedly been successfully addressed in short time spans. This list does not imply any consistent correlation between the time taken in the particular report and the time necessary for clients in general, but gives an account of some clinical claims and a sense of the *possibilities* of time-limited counselling.

therapists. Table 4.1 shows some of the claims of time-limited work with different client conditions.

Mahrer (1988) and many other experientially-oriented therapists generally reject the use of diagnostic labels to indicate who will and will not benefit from their therapies, and discount as unsuitable only those clients who themselves decline to accept or persist with their methods. Many therapists regard their clients in terms of having *multiple* problems which may be addressed, as in cognitive therapy, by composing and working systematically through a problem list, even in quite short-term therapy (see Dryden, 1995). Horowitz et al. (1984) emphasise the significance of personality traits of clients in brief therapy and therapeutic responses geared to these, arguing that reasonably flexible personalities on the whole respond better to brief treatment.

There is some evidence that brief psychodynamic therapists apply more stringent criteria to the assessment of potential clients for brief treatment than, for example, practitioners of cognitive–behaviour therapy (Budman and Gurman, 1988). Even among different forms of brief dynamic therapy there are discrepancies in selection criteria (Crits-Cristoph and Barber, 1991). This suggests a concern on the part of individual therapists and their particular orientations as to whether their approaches will fit certain clients; it does not indicate whether clients will or will not benefit from one form or another of brief or time-limited therapy or counselling. Coren (1996) suggests that we may divide views into the conservative (brief therapy suits only certain well-defined groups) and the radical (brief therapy may be tried with a wide variety of groups). Garfield (1995) places himself among the liberals and cites the view of Wolberg (1965) that it is best to assume that short-term therapy is suitable for everyone until proven otherwise.

As with psychotherapy generally, it is important for us to ask in the context of time-limited counselling which kind of approach, highlighting which variables, will most benefit each client. Rather than long-term versus short-term, psychodynamic versus behavioural, individual therapy versus group, and so on, we might address ourselves to the question of optimal matching. To some extent Rosen (1990: 65) approaches the spirit of what I have in mind. Having discounted certain severe conditions, he suggests that a combination of behavioural treatment and brief psychotherapy could best address phobic disorders, obsessive–compulsive neurosis and sexual disorders. He further recommends that brief therapy is the primary approach for anxiety states, depressive reactions, and (for short-term focal help) personality disorders. Lazarus and Fay (1990) and Lazarus et al. (1991) suggest that it is not the traditional diagnostic categories which should guide our thinking on who is suitable for brief therapy but the more comprehensive, tailored assessment made in multimodal therapy. Such assessments may include diagnostic criteria but also incorporate factors of personality, modality orientation and therapist–client fit. Thus, Lazarus has declared that in certain cases he will refer clients on – for better and/or more rapid and efficient therapy – to other practitioners when he recognises his own limitations (Dryden, 1991).

Some fallible guidelines

In the light of the above, it is appropriate to put forward some tentative suggestions as to, first, which clients might be especially suited to time-limited counselling and, secondly, which clients might be especially unsuited to it, or who may require special consideration. Readers must decide for themselves – on the basis of their own experience, theoretical orientation, clinical setting and predominant client group – to what extent they hold either a conservative or radical position on client suitability (Coren, 1996).

1   Who will benefit from time-limited counselling?

(a) People who perceive their concerns as quite circumscribed   I may be experiencing a period of particular stress at work, perhaps I am considering a career change, or I am unsure whether the academic course of study I am engaged in is the right one for me. Although sometimes underlying dynamics may be present in such cases, I disagree with those therapists who insist that there are always or usually such dynamics and that they must be explored. For many people, counselling and therapy represents an opportunity to offload, to throw out ideas and have them reflected back, to be listened to seriously, and even to receive advice. Help-seeking in these cases is related to a temporary – even momentary – dilemma, often about a well-defined issue. Psychopathology is not involved, or is not part of the helpseeker's picture at this time.

(b) People who wish to sample counselling without commitment
Since the concept of client commitment is taken so seriously by counsellors and lack of commitment is often a major barrier to successful outcomes, counsellors sometimes mistakenly try to insist on commitment. Some will only take on a client who contracts for a minimum number of sessions. But why should clients be forced to commit themselves in advance? An alternative proposition is that each session can be regarded as a valid unit of counselling or therapy. Such a practice is indeed endorsed by the experiential psychotherapist Mahrer (1988) and family therapists

Boscolo and Bertrando (1993). Elton Wilson (1996) discusses the possible usefulness of what she terms a mini-commitment.

(c) Those whose problems or preoccupations are in the mild to moderate band We know that depression is the number one mental health problem and that it presents in varying degrees of severity. Whether you accept it or not, there is a strong argument that very severe depression may yield only to appropriate medication, perhaps accompanied by some form of talking therapy. Dokter (1996) is one of a growing number of therapists – in this case a dramatherapist – who believe that chronic depression can be partly helped by brief psychological therapy. But many clients and counsellors strongly believe that for mild to moderate depression counselling or psychotherapy is the approach of choice.

In terms of grasping the range of most commonly presented problems, it is useful to look at Roberts's (1995b) survey of issues dealt with by American crisis centres. In this survey of 578,793 clients, depression is followed by substance abuse, suicide attempt, marital maladjustment, behavioural crisis, homelessness, problems of sexuality, psychiatric emergency, woman abuse, child abuse, rape trauma victims, victims of violent crime and vehicular accident victims.

(d) Those who are open to focal work One way of looking at the question of suitability is to assume that everyone may be suitable to some extent. Instead of rigorous assessment prior to a first session, it is worth considering rapid assessment and perhaps 'trial therapy' (Davanloo, 1990) within the first session. Whatever form of assessment you may use, it is possible to adapt it to some sort of practicable skeletal assessment and to build on it immediately. Hence, Arnold Lazarus can be seen using a multimodal assessment and tentative therapy within little more than half an hour in the video entitled *Kathy*. In a very short, focused period, Lazarus traverses all seven modalities, elicits one or two workable goals and has his client ready to try out some concrete new actions. Now, something like this can, potentially, be adapted for work with every client. For someone who is badly psychologically damaged, it still may be possible to conduct a sensitive, rapid (good enough) assessment, to elicit one or two modest goals and

to set to work on these. See also Dryden (1992) and Talmon (1990).

(e) People who are well motivated and ready Most therapists and counsellors enjoy working with well motivated clients, who are likely to be rewarding in either short- or long-term therapy. It is an escapable fact that such clients, probably fairly stable, perhaps very articulate, often present the best prospects for successful therapy. But there are also people whose motivation and commitment is of recent origin, perhaps born of crisis or major life events, who are not necessarily classical therapy clients. For example, a middle-aged man finds himself divorced, unhappy at work and entering counselling for the first time; he is not seeking major psychological surgery and does not need it. What he wants and is ready for is a concentrated dose of serious reflection, aided by a serious counsellor. What he wants is to think hard and feel deeply, albeit in a short space of time, about the point he has reached in his life and where he goes from here. A client like this may need only one session: he is motivated from within and is ready to make his own changes.

2   *Who may not benefit from time-limited counselling?*

(a) People who seek immediate gratification and insist that brief therapy must deliver rapid results A criticism often made of long-term therapy is that it encourages dependency or attracts people who have basic dependent characteristics. If we can rely on and extrapolate from the findings of Greenberg and Bornstein (1989), it may be that women tend to utilise therapeutic services in a more dependent manner than men. The converse of this criticism and tendency may be that certain clients will be attracted to time-limited counselling because they are denying their dependency needs and wish to opt for brisk therapy that may not touch their real, underlying problems. This may be especially true for some men. In addition, some may unconsciously expect or demand instant 'feeding' or a quick fix. In some cases they may indeed get this, or believe that they have received what they need, or they may apparently be helped rapidly only to relapse and experience deep disappointment later. The time-limited counsellor can attempt to develop a nose for this problem, but

may also consider offering clients follow-up opportunities, information on other sources of help or pertinent reading material.

(b) Those whose lives are already overly busy and hurried   I am not suggesting that these people cannot be helped by brief therapy or that they should not be offered it. The point is, rather, that an active style of counselling which includes homework assignments and perhaps a certain pressure to change (or what may be perceived as an agenda to change) may be contra-indicated. Counselling could easily become simply another part of such a person's busy lifestyle. The client may expect 'greased' counselling in his or her busy schedule in much the same way that people expect fast food. Time-limited counsellors presumably do not wish to reinforce the kind of hurry sickness that has been associated with high blood pressure, heart disease and other health problems (Adam, 1995). However, such clients might respond to strategies promising to expand their repertoire of relaxation skills (Harp, 1990; Palmer and Dryden, 1995).

(c) Those who are severely damaged and unsupported   Without categorising such clients according to *DSM IV (Diagnostic and Statistical Manual of Mental Disorders* – see APA, 1995) criteria, for example, it is relatively easy to identify who has deeply entrenched character problems, whose depression is severe, and who has been exposed to multiple abuse and trauma. If, in addition to this, these clients live isolated lives with few interests or resources, the chances are that little durable change may be achieved in short-term therapy. Unfortunately many such people do sometimes present themselves at free and sympathetic community counselling centres, hoping for miraculous transitions or for better and longer-term help and support than is available. Sometimes, clients who first appear to be reasonably strong and able to cope with demanding short-term therapy, may belatedly manifest signs of unmanageable, or hard to manage, distress. Where extended contracts cannot be offered to support these clients, sensitive referral is essential.

(d) Those unwilling to collaborate or to accept responsibility
Since a rapid working alliance and a commitment to active im-mersion in counselling are predictive of good outcomes, clients who present as oppositional, who are disposed to extreme

mistrust, who are particularly passive or inclined to engage in denial, seem unlikely to make progress. Of course, you may wonder why such clients seek counselling at all. It is sometimes because they have been sent or have certain hidden agendas (e.g. seeking leniency from a court of law), or because they habitually look for a fight in order to prove just how unlovable or irredeemable they are. Clients like these may be best directed to specialist agencies or to practitioners who have relevant experience, if you do not have it yourself. Sometimes they are helped by skilful paradoxical therapeutic techniques (Cummings and Sayama, 1995).

(e) People who have an extensive personal growth agenda It probably goes without saying that for those people who ambitiously or desperately wish to address deeply and extensively many aspects of their past, recurrent patterns of distress, and other personal and transpersonal growth agendas, short-term time-limited counselling is unsuitable. Those training as therapists and counsellors, for example, or in other ways affiliated with the human potential movement, are unlikely to seek short-term counselling. However, it would be possible for them to use time-limited counselling to look at certain *aspects* of their lives in short-term work; and for those who have had over-long, unsatisfactory experiences of therapy, a trial of focused, time-limited counselling might be helpful. Conversely, some may wish to begin with short-term commitments and graduate to longer-term contracts (Elton Wilson, 1996). Kramer (1989) notes that brief therapy can provide a useful behavioural 'push' for already well-analysed people (including therapists) who need action not insight at this stage in their lives.

It must be remembered that who is suitable for time-limited counselling is a question that relates to the orientation, intensity and length of counselling. For example, one person may benefit from 11 sessions of rational emotive behaviour therapy (Dryden, 1995) yet would not benefit from the longer, affectively challenging dynamic psychotherapy of Davanloo (1990), and vice versa. Ideally, clients opting for short-term counselling rather than crisis intervention should receive some assessment of their suitability for certain orientations of counselling, or at least for the therapeutic modalities indicated to be most helpful to them

(Lazarus, 1989). Given our present state of knowledge and training standards, however, perhaps the best we can aim for is practitioners who are honest, conscientious, flexible and experienced enough to offer each client suitably individualised time-limited counselling (Garfield, 1995; Cummings and Sayama, 1995).

5

Key Ingredients, Skills and Strategies

I am not discussing an approach-specific model of time-limited counselling and what is written here must be adapted to whatever approach the reader does espouse. What follows in this chapter might be called a common factors brief therapy approach (Garfield, 1989, 1995). Also, the matter of whether the counselling you offer is limited to two, six, twelve or twenty sessions is an important consideration. Practitioners of cognitive analytic therapy, for example, place a particular emphasis on assessment, on paperwork exercises and reformulations, and, often working to an expected 16 sessions, have a sense of a certain pattern and dynamics in the therapeutic relationship. In CAT, CMT and similar planned therapies, it can be predicted that certain ingredients will generally feature.

The key ingredients concentrated upon here are those attitudes, skills and interventions which have been found useful across the board of therapies and which I, in my work, have found clinically significant. Readers will naturally find some of these more helpful and pertinent to their own way of working than others. I have not produced an exhaustive list but one which highlights the need for clarity, collaboration, activity, responsibility, awareness of the use of time, and openness to the possibility of healthy change in a short time. You may also wish to consult Dryden and Feltham (1992) and Cooper (1995).

Decide what you, your agency and your clients mean by time-limited counselling

It is easy to assume that if the agency in which you work has a policy that only eight sessions may be offered, and you accept this and carefully explain it to your clients, then everyone is clear about the contract within which they are working. I am assuming at this point that you are not offering time-limited counselling in private practice, where you would normally have the discretion to offer time-unlimited counselling.

Certain agencies or clinical settings may offer time-limited therapy to clients who have been on a waiting list, for example, on the understanding that therapeutic time is precious and that, once embarked upon, the full three, eight or sixteen sessions must be completed. This is a very different message from that given by an agency which promises prompt appointments, offers *up to* eight sessions, and accepts that many clients use only one, two, three or four sessions. In this latter scenario, it can be argued that what is really being delivered is a kind of crisis counselling or crisis intervention, even if it becomes protracted crisis work when clients use all eight sessions. As a practitioner you need to think hard about this – are you providing and promoting 'only eight sessions' or 'up to eight sessions' or 'an intensive and structured therapy elegantly contained within eight sessions'? What is conveyed by agency literature? What is understood by clients?

Readers interested in exploring the differences between crisis intervention and short-term, time-limited counselling, might consult Aguilera (1990), Roberts (1995a) and Flegenheimer (1982: 177–92). Freeman (1968) suggests that maturational crises, role transition crises and accidental crises may all be tackled typically within six sessions. Table 5.1 depicts one version of the most salient differences claimed between crisis work and brief therapy.

There is often a grey area too, or a slippery slope, contained in words and phrases like '*normally* eight sessions' or 'eight sessions at a time'. Is there a clear limit or isn't there? If there is some discretion, who decides this and on what grounds? Is the time limit agreed mutually; is it initiated by the counsellor or, perhaps in some cases, by the client? If a client at the termination of eight sessions, for example, is in crisis and has no alternative service available, what is to happen? These questions should be faced from the outset and, where practicable, policies made. Too often counsellors are placed, by their agencies or management, in the position of having to make arrangements 'on the hoof' because the implications of anomalous client needs have not been anticipated. I am not suggesting that an absolutely watertight contract

Table 5.1 *Comparison of crisis intervention with brief psychotherapy*

	Crisis intervention	Brief psychotherapy
Selection	Any diagnosis; must be in crisis – no other selection criteria	Mild to moderate neurosis; mild personality disorder; specific selection criteria
Onset	Recent	Can be long-standing
Focus	Immediate stress	Core conflict
Goal	Restore homeostasis; promote mastery	Symptom amelioration; promote more adaptive coping mechanisms
Technique	Supportive: promotes defenses; may be directive; rarely interpretive	Confronting: removes defenses; nondirective; interpretive
Structure of therapy	Flexible: rapid onset of treatment; one-to-one plus others; sessions of variable length and frequency	Structured: extensive evaluation period; one-to-one; sessions of standard length; one session per week
Transference	Initially regressed; transference interpretations rarely used	Level of regression controlled; transference interpretations common
Termination	When crisis resolved, usually 6–10 sessions; may have time limit; termination issues often not discussed	At end of time limit or when conflict resolved, usually 12–30 sessions; termination issues often discussed

Reproduced with permission from Jason Aronson Inc. From Flegenheimer, W.V. (1982) *Techniques of Brief Psychotherapy.*

can or should be presented to every client, but a very *clear* understanding by counsellor and client alike should exist. Some agencies clearly offer six sessions with the option to contract for a further six sessions, and so on, if necessary. This arrangement takes into account that time is limited but sensibly allows for flexibility to respond to individual needs (Goss, 1995). Elton Wilson (1996) describes an extendable but tightly contracted model of therapy.

Do not fall into the trap of telling clients that their counselling will be time-limited without exploring what this means to them. It can sound like 'this is all you deserve' or 'this is all these mean funders will provide' or 'this is all you're ever going to get so you'd better make the most of it'. It can come across as perse-cutory or as selling people short. An alternative message could be: 'We have up to eight sessions together which we can use according to your need, staggering them if that is better for you, for example; but perhaps you'd like to come two or three times first so that you can get the feel of it, and then we might discuss how it fits your expectations.' In other words, remember to explore what time-limited means to each client and do not assume that your view of it is shared by every client. A sample statement for clients is given in Appendix 3. This is not an ideal model but a starting point, and you may wish to adapt it to suit your agency policies and style.

Clarify your attitude to time-limited counselling

I know counsellors whose habitual and preferred way of working is open-ended. However, if you work in private practice, for example, but times are hard and you take some part-time work in a community mental health agency, you may be required to limit the number of sessions you provide. Probably you will readily agree to this (otherwise you will not be offered the work!) but you may have inner reservations and doubts. How can adequate therapeutic work be done, incorporating transference work, in such a short time? How can a client with long-standing personal problems possibly be helped within so few clinical sessions? Obviously a completely sceptical or even hostile attitude will not be effective and is likely to communicate itself to your clients. It seems unlikely that anyone would maintain this attitude. Much more likely is an attitude of reasonable doubt and caution: I'm not sure how I can settle into a therapeutic relationship and begin serious work in such a short time but I'll have a go. I can see that these clients have no realistic alternative and something is probably better than nothing.

Perhaps the most common practice for those practitioners unfamiliar with time-limited work is to attempt simply to do less of the same. In other words, the psychodynamic counsellor will do what he or she usually does, but in a more rationed manner; the person-centred counsellor will perhaps begin to create the core conditions, but with a sense that the clock is ticking hard. Many practitioners intuitively practise in a more focused and active way and, in effect, teach themselves the art of time-limited counselling. Some, however, practise in the way they are used to practising and work at the same pace, only to find that they have arrived – without any resolution – at the final session. Some-times there may be inner reservations along the lines of: 'I can only do my best; I can't hurry myself or the client; if they're left high and dry at the end, it's the fault of the system'. Counsellors need to ask themselves to what extent they are willing to learn new skills and to adapt their approach. If, covertly, you are resisting the time constraints imposed by an agency, this will have a detrimental effect on clients. Successful time-limited work almost certainly requires hope, flexibility and a degree of eclecticism.

The opposite attitude problem is found in those practitioners who may naively or over-enthusiastically embrace short-term work by using gimmicky techniques, hurrying their clients into superficial results, generating a climate of shallow positive thinking and suppressing clients' doubts about their real progress or their misgivings about their counsellors' performance (see Regan and Hill, 1992). It is quite possible to identify clients' strengths and harness their hopes in such a way that short-lived, superficial results are achieved that are transiently satisfying for both client and counsellor. This is quite easily facilitated when clients are overly compliant, for example.

The optimal attitude for effective time-limited counselling is, I would argue, one of openness to possibilities, willingness to explore some of the techniques offered by approaches other than one's own and commitment to action research with clients, and to familiarising oneself with literature on time-limited work. In general, the counsellor who is willing to take an active approach, to be focused and realistic (non-perfectionistic), and who is always concerned with the overarching ethical question of how best to relieve suffering, is likely to be an effective practitioner in the time-limited sphere.

In the words of Angela Molnos:

> In short-term psychotherapy, be it brief dynamic psychotherapy or short-term analytic group, the therapist or the group conductor cannot afford to have or harbour any of the doubts or prejudices against brief therapies . . . The therapist has to be confident and convinced that it is possible to use the limited time to maximum effect. . . . This positive basic attitude towards the task is at least as important as is the therapist's technical ability to perform it. (1995: 52)

Be conscious of your first impressions of the client

Your first contact with a new client may be on the telephone, in person or even in a letter; or it may be through the medium of an agency report containing other practitioners' impressions, diagnoses, and so on. The client, or potential client, has already formed impressions based on his or her own needs, wishes, anxieties and any word of mouth or written information about your service. Part of your task may be to unravel and explore some of these impressions but what I want to focus on here is the practitioner's own first impressions.

A telephone caller, for example someone contacting a free employee counselling service, may well speak immediately to a counsellor who is prepared to listen to them and engage in telephone counselling without further ado. Alternatively, the call may be a brief one involving minimal discussion of access to the service, with a prompt appointment being made. The client may first talk in crisis fashion or with ambivalence, before deciding to make an appointment. He or she may be given an appointment with the counsellor on duty when they called. If you are in this position you will be in possession of certain clues from an early stage. The client may have exhibited great anxiety, obsessional characteristics, sadness, compliance, timidity or other states or traits. He or she may have used certain words or phrases repeatedly, which later turn out to carry significance. Whether or not you record such conversations on paper, an impact is made on you that can be useful to reflect upon later and it is certainly useful consciously to practise the art of rapidly homing in on first clues. According to Talmon (1990) this pre-session attunement is crucial.

When the client arrives for a first appointment, many clues are given before or besides those of a verbal nature. Is the client early, late or dead on time? Molnos (1995: 49) argues that transference is present from the first moment, manifested in the client's manner of presenting him- or herself. What is she wearing? What is his demeanour? Does she look at you directly or stare at the ground? Does he offer his hand in greeting? What degree of initiative or hesitancy is shown? Where does the client choose to sit and in what manner do they sit (slumped, upright, on the edge of the chair)? The first moments of the therapeutic relationship are rich in information. Whether this information is interpreted psychodynamically or not, it should not be overlooked.

You may or may not have explored meditation, but the meditative ability to slow down, to suspend your thinking and to concentrate fully on the object, vista or person in front of you is extremely useful (Harp, 1990). Can you take in this person's unique behaviour, their facial signals, their aura? Sometimes you can be aware of a whole history of suffering, struggle, sadness or humour in someone's face. Doing time-limited counselling does not mean that you are preoccupied with the use of time to the exclusion of noticing who or what is in front of you! Hobson (1985: 163–81) discusses the first five minutes of a meeting with a client, and I recommend as an exercise (this can be done in a training setting or alone) that you practise consciously recalling brief encounters: what was said, what the other person looked like, wore, conveyed, and so on. How vividly can you recall these encounters?

Maria told the counsellor on the telephone that she had to visit the dentist just before seeing him, had one or two dental problems and, therefore, 'might not look too pretty'. George, the counsellor, noticed through his window Maria arriving for her appointment and thought she looked older than he had expected. As they sat down to begin the counselling, George found himself pulled between thinking how fresh, fit and attractive Maria seemed, yet simultaneously how grey, resigned and shabby. In fact, she was in her late 50s and complained that life had passed her by. Since the age of 18, when she left home, she felt she had simply been swept along without any ownership of her life. She had gone through the motions, getting married and doing what she imagined she was supposed to do. Only when it had all gone very wrong, culminating in the tragic death of a son, did Maria feel a strong enough resolve to question it all. George was struck, as he pictured Maria in his mind after the first session, that in some sense she was still 18 – rather naive, lacking worldly wisdom, waiting still to be told how to live.

Often hard to focus upon and to recall, perhaps, is your first impression of the encounter itself. What did it feel like to meet this person for the first time? Did he look as you had expected him to? Did you and she look at each other comfortably? Was there a sense that you liked each other? Were you reminded of anyone? Can you guess at what your looks and demeanour meant to the client? Was rapport immediately evident or did silence and discomfort predominate? Did you immediately feel somewhat hopeful, challenged, downcast, or what? Of course, your reactions will have been a mixture of personal prejudice, good character judgement, clinical perspicacity and countertransference, and will be coloured by the unique tone of the particular encounter and the outcome of the initial session. The better we know ourselves (and psychotherapy is not necessarily the only or best method of self-knowledge), the better we may be able to discriminate between our own 'stuff' and what the client is presenting – verbally and non-verbally, consciously and unconsciously. The more self-possessed we are or, to put it differently, the more presence we are imbued with in these first meetings, the better it augurs for a fruitful outcome. In time-limited counselling there is obviously less opportunity to put things right that have started poorly at this early stage.

Forge immediate bonds and build on them

Since a massive amount of research in counselling and psychotherapy confirms that relationship factors play a highly significant part in the success of all therapies, it is essential that the time-limited counsellor heeds this. Although there is less time in which to establish trust and to get to know each other, it may be possible to find means other than gradual warming to secure trust and confidence. Curtis (1981) suggests that we direct ourselves to the importance of greetings, providing undivided attention, demonstrating expertise, being active, accepting clients' negative feelings, being appropriately protective, modelling Socratic self-discovery, and showing enthusiasm and self-confidence. At any rate, if 30 per cent of outcome variance is due to common (relationship) factors across all therapies (Lambert, 1992), the time-limited counsellor cannot afford to ignore this. Most practitioners assume that they offer high levels of acceptance, genuineness and empathy, as advocated by Rogers and others. But how can you know that you are doing this and, if you are, can you build on it and increase your relational effectiveness?

There is now ample evidence that clients are highly sensitive to how understanding, accepting, warm and helpful their counsellors or therapists are. They are also naturally alert to evidence or perception of aloofness, coldness, patronising tendencies, the therapist imposing an agenda or the therapist withholding something useful. You need to consider: (a) how your theoretical orientation colours the interpersonal impact you make; and (b) how your own personality affects the therapeutic relationship. These issues are likely to operate at conscious and unconscious levels, so that what you believe to be necessary, traditional neutrality, for example, the client perceives as unhelpful aloofness; or what you consider to be an open and friendly attitude may be experienced by your client as sloppy and unprofessional. I am not advocating the development of some impossibly demanding ability to adopt exactly the right manner for optimal bonding, but promoting an awareness of how these factors may waste time. As we have seen, a reasonably active approach is needed in short-term work, and part of this may helpfully include active bonding. By attempting to tune in to each client's preference for certain interpersonal styles, using small talk if necessary, elaborate or relaxed preambles, contracting and reviewing, you will enhance the odds of making a rapid alliance. As advocated in Dryden and Feltham (1994), it may be helpful to include fairly frequent, if brief, reviews with the client so that your work is evaluated as it proceeds.

Do not confuse bonds with collusion or avoidance of challenge, of course. In approaches such as those of Davanloo (1990) and Molnos (1995) a high level of challenge from the outset is advocated.

Consider your clients' temporal assumptions

Your clients may or may not have views about counselling and how long it will take but everyone has implicit or explicit views about time and change. Consider the following possibilities:

1 I suppose there's no time like the present.
2 I don't think I can get through another week like this.
3 Every day is the same.
4 I don't think I'll *ever* get over it.
5 I've *always* been like this.
6 It was a long time ago; I can't remember it; it's not relevant.
7 I'm not ready for this.
8 I'm too old to learn that.

9   Perhaps things will fall into place one day.
10 How long will I feel like this?

Readers will observe that most of these statements betray negative beliefs about the possibility of change; many of them indicate an attitude of powerlessness, depression, half-heartedness, vagueness and avoidance. On the one hand, distorted beliefs about the inevitability of the past overshadowing and dictating the present, and the future being inevitably frightening, are common in depression and anxiety; on the other hand, infantile amnesia (not being able to recall the past) and procrastination are very common phenomena. Broadly speaking, depression usually relates to the past (especially to loss) and anxiety to the future (especially to fear of certain situations; *see* Blackburn and Davidson, 1990). But whatever degree of disturbance or unhappiness the client experiences, he or she will always have some temporal assumptions which relate to their problems and concerns in counselling.

It is not necessary and may not be efficient to assess clients' temporal assumptions formally. This can be done to some extent, however, by using a self-assessment questionnaire such as that shown in Table 5.2. This can be used before or during time-limited counselling and may well provide useful information for counsellor and client to look at. (Note that some questions are paradoxical or provocative.) But even without the use of such devices it is often possible and useful for the counsellor mentally to register what each client's approach to time is. Sometimes this is revealed in the kinds of statement given in the list above. Often it becomes quite obvious within a very few sessions if the client is placing a large wedge of temporal safety and postponement between his or her stated goals and willingness to take some action towards them. Sometimes prolonged silences or conversational circularity within sessions alert the counsellor to how ready for change the client is. In certain cases clients may claim to be ready and willing but their actions tell another story. In yet further cases, there are clients who are impulsive, who seek instant gratification and show little insight. All such dynamics may be observable. When you are uncertain, however, or when it would be helpful to be explicit about matters, disclose your observations and seek clients' views. For example: 'You seemed very motivated when we first met; your aims appeared to be very clear. Now that we've met four times, you seem less sure, more hesitant. I wonder

Table 5.2 *Time-limited counselling: client temporal attitudes/self-assessment*

1 The thing I most urgently want to work on and change is . . .

2 I've had this problem in one form or another since . . .

3 I want it to last for another . . .

4 I suspect that what I'm not yet ready or willing to face is . . .

5 I can change my behaviour tomorrow but the reason I couldn't maintain that change is that . . .

6 I can try and change the way I think and act but I can't change the way I feel because . . .

7 Something I don't ever want to change in my life is . . .

8 What I'm losing out on by hanging on to my old habits, procrastination and fear is . . .

9 My favourite ploy for talking myself out of change and avoiding things is . . .

10 I expect counselling to help me significantly within . . .

11 One thing I can do within the next week to make at least a small change is . . .

12 Something I will do tomorrow to make a positive change is . . .

13 I'm prepared to commit myself, to make tremendous effort and endure great discomfort to effect change, but . . .

14 The best thing my counsellor can do to help me maintain and accelerate my progress is . . .

15 The time I felt/feel at my bravest/most willing to take risks was/is . . .

16 One thing I can do immediately and without anyone's help is . . .

17 What could totally, instantly transform the way I feel is . . .

18 The difference between forgiving myself for not changing and making excuses for myself is that . . .

19 I am certain that 20 years from now I . . .

20 As I finish these questions and carry on with my life, the 10 most obvious things I encounter that diminish my happiness are . . .

if that's how you see it?' Or: 'I notice that you frequently use the phrase "Maybe things will be different one day". That sounds somewhat helpless.'

By openly challenging clients' attitudes to time and change you are likely to: (a) clarify any misunderstandings between you, and

(b) maintain useful temporal pressure on the client. It is important to stress that useful means just that – repeated, clumsy attempts to hurry the client up will obviously not be useful. Temporal empathy (understanding time from the client's frame of reference) is called for and must be balanced by a positive regard for realistic time constraints (for example, whatever the client may ideally need, he or she may only be able to get six sessions). It is often useful to establish why the client is seeking counselling at this particular time, and to ask questions about how long problems have persisted and so on.

Create expectancy from the word go

How do clients approach counselling in the setting where you work? What kinds of hopes and fears do they harbour? There is considerable literature on this. Howe (1989), for example, argues that there is problem anxiety relating to the actual issues which upset clients, and service anxiety which relates to the way in which the counsellor and the agency are perceived, based both on reality and fantasy. So, clients always have some sort of expectancy which contains within it some degree of anxiety; and anxiety, as we know, contains both discomfort and arousal, or readiness to meet challenges. Indeed, Sifneos (1972), Mann (1973), Davanloo (1990) and many other brief psychodynamic therapists set out deliberately to ignite and utilise the client's anxiety for therapeutic purposes. Molnos (1995) suggests – along with other brief psychodynamic therapists – that anxiety forms one part of the triangle of defence, anxiety and true feeling, and that it is often necessary to challenge defences vigorously from the very beginning, thus triggering therapeutically-directed anxiety.

Exactly how do you create expectancy? Remembering that when potential clients first make contact they are by definition both anxious and hopeful, listen for the hope. Someone who says 'I'm really mixed up and I need help' signifies the possession of some insight and implied hope. 'You sound as if you've thought this through a bit already and have some idea that counselling could help you', could be part of an appropriate response. 'I'm glad you called when you did. It sounds as if you're serious about getting help and I'm certainly interested in meeting you and seeing how we can work on this together' conveys both hope and the prospect of a good collaboration. There are many variants of such responses, of course.

Do not mistake expectancy for promise, however. It would be unwise to say, for example, 'I've counselled many people in your position and I can guarantee that you'll feel 100 per cent better after two or three sessions with me.' For one thing, individuals are so variable that no matter how experienced and skilful you are, you cannot be sure of always getting quick and positive results. For another, if you make such a clear positive promise you risk failing and, potentially, becoming the target of a law suit. Guard against inviting superficial client compliance too. Reviews in which you probe for this should help to unearth instances of non-therapeutic compliance.

The opposite pitfall is to understate your hope and skill. If you strain not to convey any of your own hopes and to come across as neutral and merely 'professional', you risk putting the client off. What you intend as therapeutically reasoned non-directiveness may be interpreted by a telephone caller as lack of real interest or doubt about being able to help. Budman and Gurman (1988) and Talmon (1990) recommend that you consciously create expectancy at the stage of an initial telephone enquiry. This can be achieved by what you say, by your tone of voice, by asking the person to make an appointment promptly, by asking them to bring certain information with them, and so on. Expectancy can also be raised by sending out a pre-counselling questionnaire. Services which maintain waiting lists may convey the need to wait in positive terms (for example, 'We recommend that you see Dr B, who is very experienced with the issues you want to look at, and she'll be available early next month.'). It is well documented that many candidates for counselling or therapy find their problems or symptoms diminishing or disappearing while they are waiting for help. In quite simple terms, you might try asking your new clients (or those you have not yet met face to face) to think carefully about what they want from counselling and how motivated they think they are (Miller and Rollnick, 1991).

Foster within-session, between-session and post-therapy activity

A characteristic of time-limited counselling, as noted by Budman and Gurman (1988), Ryle (1990) and others, is its emphasis on client activity within, between and after sessions. The long-term model of rather passive reflection, free association and dependency gives way to a model of client readiness, commitment, hard work and risk-taking.

The need for active collaboration can be established before counselling begins by requiring clients to complete brief questionnaires or read relevant introductory material or published texts. Dryden (1995: 217–23) gives an example of a booklet describing rational emotive behaviour therapy for such purposes. This need can be reinforced in your initial contracting with clients. Again, Dryden (1995: 51) gives an example of a single sheet outline on REBT which includes what can be expected from the counsellor and what the client needs to do. Remember that the more passivity you model at the outset, consciously or inadvertently, the more you may be undermining the requirement for an active approach.

Within sessions it is recommended that you use, model and elicit from clients an active, engaged, hopeful approach. Exactly how structured this is will depend partly on your orientation. Users of REBT, CAT, CMT or multimodal therapy are likely to use a high level of structure and activity from the very beginning. Intensive brief dynamic therapy approaches may launch immediately into trial therapy, characterised by early testing challenges of clients' defences. It is essential that clients are informed about your approach in advance and asked for permission to try anything that may be particularly unusual or that might be perceived as threatening. In comparison with traditionally less active or directive approaches, it is necessary for the counsellor to be somewhat more proactive and structured in time-limited work (Thorne, 1994). This means that the client's agreement to work in a certain way may need to be sought and in some cases their natural pace (if it is slow) may be challenged. But the kind of activity I refer to is also about willingness to think hard, to take risks in contacting and displaying feelings and to undertake work between sessions.

Homework is not a useful term for everyone, since it can conjure up memories of resentfully completed school tasks. It may be best to explain to clients that the typically reflective nature of the counselling session is insufficient in itself to achieve the desired change; by engaging in therapeutic work between sessions, the client is complementing their work with the counsellor. The typical counselling session is an hour in a week (168 hours) and in a time-limited contract of, say, eight hours, actual contact time with the counsellor is very small in comparison with elapsed time. It is best to convey the reality that time in 'real life' far outweighs time in counselling, and so a particular effort and commitment is called for.

Between-session work may include keeping a diary of thoughts and moods, experimenting with new behaviours, visiting significant places, unearthing old photographs, reading relevant self-help books (see below), and so on. Whatever work is negotiated, it should clearly relate to what is discussed within sessions, it should be sufficiently challenging to have therapeutic potency, and an agreement should be reached on specifics. Exactly what will the client do, when, where, with whom and why? How might the client sabotage his or her intentions to carry out the activity? It is also important to note that homework may include refraining from certain activities (drinking less, ceasing to engage in sexual behaviour, deliberately taking time out for relaxation). Busyness in itself is obviously not the aim; the goal is tasks tailored to the clients' needs and current stage of progress. Always take such tasks seriously, checking on the outcome in the following session, and helping clients to learn from gains and disappointments – of course, doing this in a manner that will not be perceived as judgemental.

The expectation that the client will work to effect changes between sessions sets the further expectation that he or she will be able and committed to engage in similar action after counselling has ended. In some cases it is appropriate to space and stagger sessions to allow for substantial self-change and experimentation on the part of the client between sessions; this sends the message that the counsellor is a consultant rather than a saviour, someone to be turned to professionally rather than depended upon chronically (Dryden, 1992: 22–37). Most writers on time-limited therapy agree that improved post-counselling autonomous behaviour is highly likely to occur in most adults and that counsellors will often not witness the fruits of their work (Budman and Gurman, 1988).

There are two main forward-looking objectives that time-limited counsellors should consider. First, the generation of expectancy and hope – even from the beginning of counselling – lays the foundations for growth. As counsellors we are in a position to implant seeds of change, new ways of looking at life, of making relationships, taking risks, and so on. Clients learn both new techniques and attitudes in counselling which they will carry with them. It has been said that the therapeutic process, however modest, is irreversible. Secondly, relapse is to be expected and should be prepared for. Without demoralising the client, it is wise to skilfully introduce the possibility of relapse: the return of symptoms, old subterfuges and the resurfacing of psychological pain. Imagery and rehearsal by role-play can be utilised to entertain relapse scenarios and to practise or consider coping strategies. It is inevitable that things will go wrong in our lives, no matter how long we have been in therapy. In short-term counselling, time should be made available for at least minimal discussion of these issues. If homework and behavioural rehearsal seem alien to your approach, see Mahrer's (1988) humanistic way of tackling these matters. See also Dryden and Feltham (1992) and Gersie (1996) for further ideas. It is helpful, too, to decide on certain books which you are prepared to recommend to clients. Below are some examples:

- David Burns (1990) *The Feeling Good Handbook*. New York: Plume. This is a big book, based on cognitive therapy, which cogently explains its principles and sets out many self-help exercises.
- Richard Carlson (1995) *Shortcut Through Therapy*. New York: Plume. The author challenges the long-term therapy model, and commends living in the here and now and adopting realistic, optimistic goals.
- Elizabeth Wilde McCormick (1990a) *Change for the Better*. London: Unwin. This book explains the principles of cognitive analytic therapy and invites readers to engage in self-help exercises.
- John Preston, Nicolette Varzos and Douglas Liebert (1995) *Every Session Counts: Making the Most of Your Brief Therapy*. San Luis Obispo, CA: Impact. This slim American volume is the first purpose-written consumer guide to optimal use of brief therapy; it offers succinct guidance to the process.
- Tom Rusk (1991) *Instead of Therapy*. Carson, CA: Hay House. In spite of the title, this is not an anti-therapy book but recommends an active, short-term, client-driven model of change which views counsellors as consultants or coaches.

Allow for the possibility of 'miracles'

Practitioners of brief solution-focused therapy utilise what they call the 'miracle question' (Cade and O'Hanlon, 1993). Essentially this device is catalytic, urging the client to imagine how their life would look if they woke up tomorrow morning, after a miracle had occurred to solve their problems. Exactly what would have changed, in detail? How would the client and others notice it? By slipping imaginally into a solution in this way, clients may find themselves actually constructing their own solution, finding within themselves the ability to identify the necessary building blocks. Now, this is *not* at all the same thing as positive thinking or pretending that things are fine when they are not. It is an exercise designed to help people recall their own solution-constructing abilities.

I want to add a slightly different dimension to this. Imagine that a miracle is occurring now; or a miracle is struggling to express itself now. Instead of thinking of a miracle as absolutely out of the ordinary, think of it as an extension of your deeper potential. Before you could swim, it was apparently impossible for you to swim. Suddenly, after some trial and error you were able to swim. You were then confident, things fell into place, something clicked in your mind and body and the miracle had happened. Somewhere beneath depression there is the capacity to be happy; somewhere beneath the phobia lies the confidence and light-heartedness to confront or ignore the fear. Frequently in counselling, neither the client nor the counsellor really believes this. Both may collude in the assumption that there must be a protracted, uphill struggle or a mysterious lengthy process. Both ignore or forget the ever-present possibility of a miracle taking place.

Miller and Rollnick (1991) argue that a decision-making process is always in operation. We can decide to remain fearful, addicted, or whatever, or we can confront our fears, drop our addictions, and so on. They cite an example from Premack (1970: 115):

A man dates his quitting smoking from a day on which he had gone to pick up his children at the city library. A thunderstorm greeted him as he arrived there; and at the same time a search of his pockets disclosed a familiar problem: he was out of cigarettes. Glancing back at the library, he caught a glimpse of his children stepping out in the rain, but he continued around the corner, certain that he could find a parking space, rush in, buy the cigarettes, and be back before the children got seriously wet. The view of himself as a father who would 'actually leave the kids in the rain while he ran after cigarettes' was . . . humiliating, and he quit smoking.

Miller and Rollnick portray this kind of event as an awareness of discrepancy or cognitive dissonance. I think of myself as a caring father but I am quite ready to let my children get soaked while I pursue my addiction. Perhaps I abhor cowardice in others but cling to my phobia or lack of assertiveness. Perhaps I believe that life is precious and that my deceased partner would have wanted me to make the most of my life, yet I sink into self-pitying depression. It is often at the point when people realise deeply just how discrepant or untenable their position is that a miracle occurs. This is also probably what Krishnamurti and Bohm (1985) mean by an instantaneous change of heart and what often characterises religious conversions.

Perhaps minor miracles at least can be facilitated by provocative ideas or visualisation. A rational emotive behaviour therapy exercise has the client (say, an agoraphobic who insists that she could not possibly leave the house alone) imagine that her children are in grave danger at a known location and only she can save them: could she leave the house alone in such circumstances? Almost certainly, the discrepancy between maternal protectiveness and agoraphobia would have to be dissolved immediately. Similarly, there are many reports of ordinary people acting heroically (out of character) in life-threatening situations.

Lazarus (1968) gave one of the earliest accounts of the technique of time-projection. The depressed client was guided into a trance state and asked to visualise enjoyable everyday scenes 24 and 48 hours in the future, then a week, a few weeks, and finally up to six months later. Between each step she was asked to savour the pleasant sensations associated with each scene. At the end she was asked, still in trance, to return to the time, six months previously, when she was depressed. She was de-hypnotised, and reported feeling much better, having gained a new perspective; the success continued in real life. (I have slightly simplified the details for the sake of brevity.) Lazarus referred to this technique as time projection with positive reinforcement, and suggested that it can be used without hypnosis with some clients. He also admits that it will not be effective for all clients.

If counselling becomes a humdrum affair based on an assumption that profound and sudden changes cannot happen (perhaps even *should not happen*) then the possibility of miracles is altogether denied. Whether we prefer to think in terms of discontinuous behaviour patterns, *satori*, peak experiences, miracles, successful time projection techniques or whatever, we do well to allow for them as an ever-present possibility. Equally, we do well to avoid encouraging what Molnos (1995) refers to as idealising the future as an escape from a painful past.

Don't waste session time

Obviously, in time-limited counselling time is short and precious. There is a certain pressure to be active, to get to the point. Time in each session is finite, however it has been contracted (30 minutes, 50 minutes, 1 hour, 2 hours, etc.) and its moment-by-moment use needs to be heeded. This does not mean, however, that counselling should become a hurried affair, something like 'greased counselling', causing clients discomfort. Rather, it suggests that unlike open-ended therapy in which the therapist can assume that themes may be returned to later because they will crop up again and again, in time-limited work the moment must be seized. Clients as well as counsellors should ideally make time count (Preston et al., 1995).

Here is an example of what I mean. The counsellor has been seeing the client for several sessions and there are only three or four left to go. In this particular session, which has been characterised by a certain unsatisfactory, meandering quality, it is already 15 minutes from the end of the session. There is a temptation, not only for an easy life but also because counsellors are trained not to open cans of worms at the very end of the session, to let the remaining time slide by and to write this session off as a necessarily low key one. However, here the counsellor feels a certain disquiet, noticing his own tendency to want to let the session run to an uneventful end. He studies his client's face, realises that the client has been saying, in effect, 'Well, you can't have everything in this life, you just have to settle for what you can get', and decides to halt this assumption. 'I think in fact that you'd like to scream out just how much you do want from life', says the counsellor. In other words, perhaps the client is a little too used to resignation, which masks a longing for love, excitement and meaningful contact with others. With only five or ten minutes to go, the counsellor takes the risk of pushing quite forcefully. 'You really do want much more than you usually admit, don't you?', asks the counsellor. In a powerful crescendo of feeling, the client allows tears of hope to show. 'We're coming to an end of this session but there's plenty of feeling left in you; don't be afraid of it', says the counsellor. The session ends on time (another client must be seen) but this client, however tearful, is better off than if the session had been allowed to slide into an expedient ending plateau.

This example should demonstrate the difference between rushed counselling which inappropriately hurries the client, and counselling which is informed simultaneously by a sense of urgency and timelessness. One way of looking at brief counselling is that the session is merely 1 hour out of 168 hours in a week and that, therefore, the client must be strongly encouraged to engage in homework assignments between sessions (Dryden and Feltham, 1992). Another perspective is that this 1 hour out of 168 is as pregnant with possibility, is as real and challenging, as the other 167 hours. Instead of backing off from taking risks in the last 10 minutes, why not regard these precious minutes as a real opportunity? Since we are quite familiar with the doorknob phenomenon (clients disclosing significant material just as it is time to go), perhaps we should learn to capitalise on this by paying particular attention to what is said or not said towards the very end of the session. Reynolds (1985) challenges the 'myth of the golden [therapeutic] hour', arguing that the *whole* of life is precious in each hour and each moment. 'Don't put your life on hold,' says Reynolds. He commends a moment-by-moment listening in the therapy hour too. Life within the therapy hour, perhaps, should not be put on hold. If we are truly *with* our clients, we share their moment-to-moment negotiations with fear and possibility. We cannot decide that the session is virtually over and that remaining feelings have to be managed or shelved.

You can add to this argument the reminder that the relationship between client and counsellor constitutes a certain co-presence. Their meeting may be regarded as something too precious for any part of it to be thrown away. We assume that we will inevitably meet again, but at any time that relationship may be suddenly ended by the accidental death of either party. (In the case of working with the dying, the imminence of death presumably adds a certain therapeutic intensity to every session.) This existentialist awareness has been highlighted by philosophers like Buber and psychotherapists like Friedman. We also often assume that we must tread carefully, but we can end up treading so carefully that the client's day never comes.

When considering the best use of session time, weigh up the advantages and disadvantages in each case of formal assessments. Practitioners are divided on this issue, with some insisting on thorough assessment in all cases, some on selective assessments only, and others preferring either minimal or no assessment. Certainly, if the time available to you is very short and the client is highly motivated, you may consider waiving formal assessment procedures. It is always important to question what degree and kind of assessment is appropriate for each client in time-limited work.

Be prepared to refer the client for help elsewhere

Maria, the client described above, had already seen one counsellor, who she decided would not be mature enough to help her ('could've been my daughter') and seemed somewhat passive. She had previously been in a women's group but found herself unable to speak freely. Although depressed and anxious, she was determined not to succumb to a regime of numbing medication. She was clearly searching for the kind of help that would be right for her. A textbook response to Maria might well have been to insist that she saw her doctor for appropriate medication and/or that she was referred for long-term analytic therapy. Yet George felt, almost in spite of himself, that she could benefit from working with him and so agreed to a counselling contract. Since Maria could not afford to pay his usual fees, he would have had even more reason to refer her on. This was a conscious decision not to refer.

When it is reasonably clear that a prospective client requires long-term therapy, medical or psychiatric assistance, or some other specialist help that you cannot offer, an ethical imperative exists. You must advise them of your assessment, regardless of whether you are in private practice and need their custom, for example. When you are obliged to work in a time-limited manner and find yourself confronted with a client who obviously or almost certainly needs long-term counselling, again you are ethically obliged, I believe, to tell them this. When there is any reason, in fact, for doubting whether you or your service is best for a particular client, you should weigh up carefully what is involved in telling them this or withholding it. A client who is highly sensitive to rejection – or inclined to interpret any hint of a referral elsewhere as rejection – needs to be managed differently from a client who is robust, resourceful and only in mild crisis.

Ideally, every counsellor and counselling agency would have exhaustive information on and access to alternative sources of help in their area. Indeed, it is highly desirable that every counsellor should keep and update such information. But there are always shortfalls in provision. I am often surprised to find that a waiting list for local NHS psychotherapy is a year long, or that no self-help group or organisation for post-traumatic stress exists, or that no one locally specialises in eating disorders, and so on. Time is obviously saved for clients if they can be pointed in the direction of the most appropriate facility or practitioner, rather than muddling along with the first counsellor they come across regardless of suitability. Counsellors too use their time most efficiently when they can identify what they do best and with which clients.

Find and work with a focus

Those approaches advocating non-directiveness and neutrality on the part of the counsellor easily fall into the trap of meandering extemporising on the part of the client. In other words, without a focus, a goal or a time limit, it is not surprising when clients ramble, regress and become dependent. Successful time-limited work is almost always focused, even if the focus is not always on explicitly specified goals. The overriding focus, for example, may be implicit and affective, with a bereaved person needing to cry about their loss, remonstrate and get things out of their system, for example. A narrower focus may be to learn to cope with being a widower, and a narrower focus still to take up new interests, to move house or make new friends. From a psychodynamic perspective, the focus may be on links between this loss and earlier losses, whereas from a cognitive–behavioural perspective it may be on counterproductive beliefs about coping and having a right to enjoy life. Most orientations adapted to short-term work agree on the need to identify a focus (Balint et al., 1972; Dryden, 1995), which also entails learning the art of skilful neglect (Malan, 1963).

In Budman and Gurman's (1988) view, it is useful to think of most clients in terms of probable interpersonal, developmental and existential foci. These include losses; developmental dys-synchronies (for example, the client has reached a certain age without accomplishing expected life tasks); interpersonal conflicts; symptomatic presentations; and personality disorders. Budman and Gurman refer to these as the five most common foci. They may not necessarily or immediately represent the client's view of why they are coming for counselling. When foci have been identified and agreed upon, goals for dealing with them may be discussed.

Clients presenting with a clearly defined goal or cluster of concerns are usually more easily helped, except when the reported symptom, say, is a defensive smokescreen or conceals a hidden agenda. In the former case, you may work on the goal presented until it becomes apparent what lies beneath the surface, then change your tactics to deal with what follows. However, when there is insufficient time to play this waiting game, you may need to press for greater candour, insight or risk-taking on the part of the client. Vigorous challenge in the style of Davanloo (1990) or Molnos (1995) may achieve the desired result. Alternatively, verbal or written explanations of how defence mechanisms operate may be used. The Psychotherapy File used in CAT (*see* Appendix 2) partly serves the purpose of educating the client in such matters.

There are two other scenarios in which finding a focus is difficult. First, the client may be too confused, vague or inarticulate to be able to describe how he or she feels and what the precise problems are. Secondly, the client may experience so many problems that it seems impossible to know where to begin. In both scenarios it is often useful to help the client narrow their thoughts down by asking for a single word or phrase that approximately summarises their most pressing concern (Lazarus, 1989). With skill, you should then be able to help the client expand on this and render it into workable material. Another way of approaching these difficulties is to ask the client to make a list of problems, either during the session or between sessions. Your task is then to guide the client in ranking them in some approximate order and to begin therapeutic work on the first one. It is helpful to work with positively phrased goals as a focus (for example, 'I want to learn to be more assertive'), but a focus like 'I just can't come to terms with what a miserable family mine is' can also lend itself to quite rapid therapeutic activity.

Since almost all texts on brief therapy insist that the work must be highly focused, it is easy to assume that it must be! It is worth considering at least one dissenting view, however. Jones et al. (1988), having conducted research into therapy of 12 sessions, came to the conclusion that while a special focus may be necessary for 'the more disturbed patient', others may be amenable to an approach allowing them to work 'on issues of central importance in an emerging, if unplanned, fashion'. Such an approach is advocated by these authors as well as by Horowitz et al. (1984). It is also important to bear in mind that you may, with the best intentions, persuade your client to develop what initially seems the most obvious focus but later turns out not to be the best entry point to therapy. Remember too that some clients may compliantly agree on a focus simply to keep you happy.

Consider using the most obvious and least radical interventions

Many counsellors and psychotherapists are trained in 'depth' approaches which imply a lengthy and radical overhaul of the personality of their clients. Many, too, are temperamentally attracted to working in this way and to regarding time-limited work as merely symptom-removal, as only dealing with the presenting problem, manifest content and secondary process. Yet many clients actually seek symptom-removal and are mainly concerned with overcoming their present crisis. This mismatch of expectations parallels the religious practice and conviction of offering food and shelter to the hungry so that they may be attracted and hopefully converted to the 'real' message of the saviour. Some examples of this mismatch in counselling are given by Patten and Walker (1990) and Williams (1994).

Unfortunately a great deal of training still focuses on underlying personality dynamics and discusses clients' concerns in terms of their manifest content and what is beneath this, and many counsellors are, quite naturally, fascinated by this approach. The ordinary people who seek counselling are often quite uninterested, however, in such theories or in the pursuit of anything other than the extinction of painful problems in the present. There is a danger that the stress, redundancy, divorce or other situation which brings the client to counselling may be treated with some disdain. A client presenting with acute stress reactions, for example, may benefit most from some explanation of how stress operates and from simple relaxation and assertiveness training. Indeed, Lazarus (1989) advocates identifying just such presenting concerns and the most compelling remedies for them. Often enough, as many student or employee counsellors can testify, clients appreciate a single session simply to get something off their chest, to be listened to, to bounce ideas off, and so on. The counsellor may be used like a touchstone. Learn to recognise when this is the case instead of foisting your therapeutic ambitions on every client. Even in longer-term brief therapy (*see*, for example, Malan, 1963), focal concerns are respected and 'over-determination', characterised by the therapist's perfectionism, is regarded as counterproductive. Malan refers to a need for skilful neglect of certain areas of functioning that, however interesting, would delay matters if they were investigated.

Opting for non-radical interventions causes some anxiety in certain practitioners who fear that they will be responsible for a flight into health, for symptom substitution, and so on. Cathartic ventilation of feelings, seeking advice and normalising feedback, being referred elsewhere, being taught how to breathe into a paper bag, suggesting that the client reads self-help books – these are all strategies that may be extremely helpful to clients. I am not suggesting that strategies like these be uncritically resorted to as a matter of course with all clients. Rather, it is always worth considering providing the client with what he or she wants or needs directly. You can at the same time suggest that deeper issues *might* be involved (or might not be) and that the client could choose now or later to investigate deeper or more complex issues. What you obviously cannot do in short-term counselling is to begin with the assumption that deep and long-term work is essential; and even if you tend to believe that it always is, you could be wrong!

It is necessary to add a caveat here. Some clinical experience and research suggests that the opportunity to encounter depth, to confront defences and to ventilate strong feelings is highly valued by many clients, including those whose experiences are based on short-term counselling or therapy (Cummings et al., 1995; Mahrer, 1988; Mohamed and Smith, 1996; Nichols, 1974).

Take clients' extratherapeutic factors into account

It has been calculated that up to 40 per cent of outcome variance in therapy may be related to factors peculiar to each client's everyday life and environment, social supports, chance events, existing character strengths, and so on (Lambert, 1992). If this is so, then this area is even more significant than the contribution of therapeutic relationship factors and should be taken seriously by all therapists – especially time-limited practitioners. What kinds of extratherapeutic factors should we be aware of? Below are some of them:

1 Does the client have a satisfying job and secure income?
2 Does the client live in satisfying, reasonably stress-free accommodation in a safe area?
3 Is the client surrounded by or does he or she have access to family, partners, friends and/or colleagues who are supportive?
4 Has the client suffered unduly from any major life events recently or across the lifespan?
5 Is the client reasonably physically healthy?
6 What resources does the client have in terms of intelligence, attractiveness, robustness, contacts, etc.?
7 Is the client a member of an oppressed group and does she or he have an awareness of how this impacts on them?

Peake et al. (1988) take the question of extratherapeutic factors seriously and suggest that brief psychotherapists must consider and address these factors squarely. 'The brief psychotherapist will need to make a better peace with naturally-occurring groups (e.g. synagogues, churches and community centers) in a way that promotes learned resourcefulness and combats learned helplessness' (Peake et al., 1988: 229). Other sources of extratherapeutic support mentioned by these authors include mutual aid groups like Alcoholics Anonymous. The lesson to be learned here by those wishing to work effectively and to take research findings and common sense into account is that any propensity we may have to see ourselves as therapists as clients' precious, sole source of help, must be overcome. Clients will frequently need to identify what facilitating and restraining forces exist in their own family and social contexts. To this end, therapists like Budman and Gurman (1988) willingly include family members or significant others in occasional sessions in order to cast light on certain obstacles or to cement progress.

In some cases, for example clients whose difficulties may relate to their gender, ethnicity and sexuality, there is a strong case for encouraging direct links with social support and social change groups, as advocated by the work of some brief and social therapists (Newman, 1991). While the subject of politics and therapy is beyond the scope of this book, readers may like to consider to what extent even learned resourcefulness is insufficient for particularly disadvantaged people, who may in addition need to learn political restlessness and action.

Use acceleration and intermittency

Although much of this book concerns work within a limited, linear series of clinical sessions, the use of time can and should also be considered in counselling and therapy that have no set time constraints. For example, I have worked in agencies and in private practice where there has been no apparent need to shorten counselling. However, at certain points of the therapeutic process with certain clients, it sometimes becomes apparent that the client needs or prefers a pace or style of work that calls for flexible contracting and scheduling. I will illustrate what I mean by two case examples.

James was seeing a counsellor because he had a long-standing problem with acute social anxiety. Many weeks went by during which modest progress was made. James would come and report on recent challenges and setbacks in his everyday life, he would delve into possible early antecedents to his behaviour and generally try to make inroads with insight and homework strategies. Moira, the counsellor, was quite active in this process. During a review, James admitted that he was disappointed with his progress and was becoming frustrated and somewhat angry. Moira utilised these feelings in the review session by focusing relentlessly

*on James's dissatisfaction and by getting him to dwell on the vivid
recall of certain scenes. By the end of the session Moira had
elicited James's willingness to make a contract for accelerated
change which entailed very specific, tailored homework along
cognitive–behavioural lines. Perhaps this move could not have
been made earlier; perhaps James needed to reach this impasse
which created anger. But Moira could have simply carried on
working through it, remaining with the 'stuckness', having faith
in the client's so-called process. Instead, she interpreted the
client's slowing down and dissatisfaction as a cry for a helpful
push: perhaps there is a time for allowing the client to suffer and
a time to apply necessary pressure.*

While the above case illustrates judiciously accelerated change,
the following case demonstrates that sometimes progress may be
made by heeding signs from the client that a staggered or
intermittent approach is called for.

*Angela, a highly intelligent student, had consulted a counsellor
because she was experiencing disturbing and depressing mood
changes. She had an initial, one-off session and felt much better.
Some weeks later she visited the counsellor again for a kind of
check-up, and disclosed some significant information about
herself. Following a long break, Angela again saw the counsellor
because she felt depressed. However, after just two further visits
she again felt reasonably content. During the second of these two
sessions, the counsellor had a distinct feeling that both he and
Angela were becoming a little bored, that the session had tilted
into ritual. Angela declined a further visit the following week,
saying that she would get in touch when she needed to. On
reflection, the counsellor considered that Angela was an excep-
tionally bright person for whom small doses of attention,
acceptance and reframing were quite potent. Too great a dose
of counselling (or time available for counselling) seemed
counterproductive for someone who, perhaps with homeopathic
logic, needed only tiny amounts of an active ingredient. No
objective evidence is available to support the hunch of the counsellor in this case, but he was left with the strong conviction that
for such a client the temporal assumption of regular weekly
sessions was not indicated. Intermittent counselling was the
strategy of choice (Cummings and Sayama, 1995).*

Use firm and flexible endings

An unresolved debate concerns the merits of strictly time-limited counselling versus time-rationed but flexible counselling. When I refer to firm and flexible endings I mean that they can be *either* one or the other, but may also be a judicious combination. Many of the arguments have been, or will be, outlined elsewhere in this book. You will need to consider your own and your agency's position on these factors. Here, I outline kinds of endings and how they may be dealt with.

Strictly time-limited counselling. This is decided in advance by the counsellor or agency. Whether three, six, eight or twenty sessions are offered, this policy has the advantages of predictable costs and management of time; it can be preferred by some clients and be used therapeutically to help the client confront their own resistances. It has the further advantage that therapy can be planned. The most obvious disadvantage is that some clients may not be well served by an arbitrary ending point. Even within this way of working, decisions must be made about whether counselling is offered on a strictly weekly basis; whether session dates, including a firm ending date, are fixed; whether staggered sessions are introduced; and so on. Endings can be anticipated, work on relapse management can be done, issues of loss can be worked through to some extent. Goodbye letters (Ryle, 1990) may be exchanged, or other means of separating and evaluating outcomes may be found.

Very brief counselling (one to three sessions). It is easy to overlook the very real differences between time-limited counselling of three or twenty sessions. When only one or three sessions are offered or permitted, the work will inevitably be highly focused and will often have at least an element of crisis resolution in it. The therapeutic relationship is not likely to become intimate and hard to disengage from, and a businesslike farewell may be perfectly in order. The exception to this is when a client is referred, say, to an employee assistance programme (EAP) counsellor by a third party who does not envisage any issues emerging besides those presented at assessment. An example might be an employee referred for 'stress problems' who turns out to have complex underlying conflicts. In this case, the counsellor may have to negotiate for extra sessions or make a rapid referral elsewhere. In some cases an undesirably abrupt and potentially damaging ending could ensue. This should be anticipated by (a) knowing what room for negotiation exists, and (b) maintaining an up-to-date referral file.

Time-limited but flexible counselling. This includes the following:

- A fixed number of sessions that may be distributed according to convenience and need, say 12 sessions spread over an entire year.
- A fixed number of sessions beginning weekly and tapering off by agreement to fortnightly, monthly, and so on.
- A fixed number of hours that may be arranged in any way – including, if desirable, block sessions of three hours, or more sessions, each of 30 minutes' duration.
- A fixed initial number of sessions, say six, with the possibility of a further six sessions, and so on.
- A fixed initial contract of a certain number of sessions, with the option of open-ended therapy thereafter.

These arrangements all have different rationales and implications but a common factor is negotiation. If you opt for or are permitted to use this approach, clearly you need to hone your negotiation skills and to base decisions on shared views on the client's needs and progress.

Sessionally-focused counselling. This phrase refers to the practice of assuming that each session is or may be the only session, or may be the last. No assumption is made that work is ongoing or that clients want or need more than this time. Equally, clients are given the right to decide whether they want further time later, but every subsequent session may be deemed a potential last session. This contrasts with the practice of those therapists who insist on contracting for a formal ending with a period of notice. Some practitioners may regard every session as existentially or mystically the last, based, respectively, on the possibility that the client and counsellor may never meet again and/or that future expectations are generally illusory. It should be borne in mind, of course, that there will always be a certain drop-out rate; even when time is limited to six sessions, some clients will simply not return after one, two or three sessions.

Short-term but open-door counselling. The expectation of some counsellors is that clients will attend for sessions over a short period but may well return for follow-up, booster (reinforcement), or episodic sessions over an extended time. Although farewells may still be appropriate, the course of counselling may be characterised by many hallos and goodbyes, and perhaps by periodic contact by telephone or letter.

None of these approaches is the correct or best one, but which approach is chosen will depend on practicalities, agency policies, client and counsellor factors, and chance. Be as clear as possible at the outset what clients can expect to receive, and consider the psychodynamic effects each approach may have on endings. The more explicitly time-limited your initial contract has been, and the more open a factor this has been throughout counselling (for example, by reminders about how many sessions are left from week to week), the more the end is present from the beginning. How you actually end will, of course, depend on the many factors discussed above, plus individual considerations. Chapter 7 includes a look at problems with endings. Remember too that it is useful, although often difficult, to obtain feedback from clients on their perceptions of the counselling (Goss, 1995).

6

Case Examples: Learning from Experience

In this chapter I refer to some case examples from clinical literature, followed by some relevant case vignettes, and some illustrative segments of hypothetical time-limited work. Readers are invited to consider whether certain presenting issues are better treated by time-limited counselling than others, what clinical questions are thrown up generally, what problems should be anticipated, and so on.

Cases from the literature

The most famous cases of brief therapy are probably Freud's. Katarina was seen only once, Lucy R. for nine weeks, Emmy von M. for seven weeks one year, followed by eight weeks the next year, Dora for 11 weeks. These were all reported as successful cases. Freud is said to have analysed Sandor Ferenczi in six weeks. The conductor Bruno Walter is said to have been cured of paralysis of the arm in six sessions (Sterba, 1951).

Viktor Frankl the logotherapist was already using paradoxical techniques in the 1940s. Frankl reports on a colleague achieving successes within 4 to 12 sessions, often with clients who had suffered from their phobic symptoms for many years. In one case, a man suffering from severe anxiety attacks was given two ten-minute sessions of instruction in paradoxical intention which achieved considerable improvement. Indeed, Frankl reports many similar cases and refutes the accusation that they result in relapse or symptom substitution (Frankl, 1973).

Lazarus (1958) presented perhaps one of the first succinct accounts of eclectic, time-efficient cases of therapy. In a series of 21 sessions of varying lengths and amounts overall to less than 16 hours within a period of 10 weeks, Lazarus helped this client substantially to overcome his anxiety and obsessive–compulsive problems. Most of the first four hours were devoted to history-taking, psychological testing and exploration. Lazarus used interpretation, progressive relaxation, assertiveness training, psychodramatic and hypnotic techniques. By the tenth session, each meeting was taking only 30 minutes. Eight months after termination, the client reported cessation of his compulsions and general well-being.

Mann (1973) reports on the 'case of the conquered woman', who was 'suffering from spreading phobic symptoms on the basis of well-repressed aggressive and libidinal strivings' (1973: 89), within a 12-week contract of psychoanalytically-oriented therapy. Mann's study reports on each of the sessions and concludes with a follow-up after 18 months. Mann's is one of the few approaches which is firmly time-limited.

Budman and Gurman (1988) present a transcript of a case of brief therapy of seven sessions with a man experiencing problems in close relationships stemming from the death of his wife and some possible antecedent factors in his family of origin. Budman and Gurman's model rests on an I-D-E understanding of human problems. This focuses on interpersonal, developmental and exis-tential issues. This case, or part of it, is available on tape – *Brief Therapy in Action: A Clinical Demonstration* by Simon Budman and Alan Gurman, BMA Audio Cassettes (Guilford Publications), 1988. Although this approach is not strictly time-limited, the tape demonstrates a certain pressure towards treatment brevity and discouragement of dependency.

Cases of single-session behaviour therapy are reported by Marks (1989) and McCann (1992), for agoraphobia and post-traumatic stress respectively. Palmer and Dryden (1995) report on a successful case of panic treated multimodally in one session. Talmon (1990) presents many case examples of people treated, for depression, anxiety, obesity, divorce and so on, in one session. As far as I am aware, the record for brevity of successful treatment surely goes to Andreas and Andreas (1992) who, employing neuro-linguistic programming techniques, successfully treated a woman's bee phobia of 20 years' standing in seven minutes. The case reported by Frankl (above) of a man cured of severe anxiety in two ten-minute sessions, surely comes a close second. Those inclined sceptically to dismiss the claims of the newer therapies on principle might consider the claim of the psychoanalyst, Groddeck, that he cured a woman suffering from compulsive vomiting and attendant weight loss in three quarters of an hour (Groddeck, 1951: 90).

Perhaps the record for the strangest circumstances in which single-session therapy was administered is held by the eminent logotherapist, Viktor Frankl (1985: 84), who reports on a case of (pseudo-vicarious) single-session therapy for a phobia, with a member of the Gestapo. I call it pseudo-vicarious because the Gestapo member pretended to Frankl that he needed the advice for a friend, but Frankl realised it was for the man himself.

It is worth looking closely at a case report by McCann (1992). The client had been badly burned in a mining accident, resulting in his losing both arms and requiring prosthetic shoes, as well as suffering from deafness. He had later spent nine months in a hospital, unconscious. He was haunted by flashbacks of the mineshaft in which he was temporarily trapped. For about eight years he struggled with severe symptoms of post-traumatic stress disorder, until receiving treatment using eye movement desensitisation and reprocessing (EMDR). Basically, this treatment entails recapturing distressing memories as images and holding them while the therapist repeats a number of lateral finger movements. This procedure was repeated several times with different images. This client reported gaining 'an overwhelming sense of peace' from the single session of treatment; later subjective and objective evaluations confirmed substantial and lasting progress. He was seen for a period for brief progress checks at intervals of one to three months. How can any counsellor or therapist fail to want to investigate such procedures and to compare them with their own? Although this is a single case and, therefore, not sufficient in its own right to establish the efficacy of EMDR, Shapiro (1995) gives further supportive evidence.

The above case, although dramatic, is not an isolated one in therapeutic literature. Apart from Freud's early cases, the early cases of many innovators often have an apparently dramatic character. Malan (1963) has suggested that high energy inputs and rather rapid clinical successes may characterise the work of some therapists early in their careers. But dramatic or outstanding successes may also sometimes be attributed to reversal of so-called hysterical symptoms. Grant et al. (1993) report on a woman presenting with rapidly deteriorating eyesight. Medical diagnosis confirmed a blind spot in the retina and a prognosis of total blindness was made. Yet within four sessions of therapy her vision reverted to almost normal and at the ninth and final session was completely cured. Expression of lifelong anger and the therapist's interpretation of her material by using optical metaphors partly accounts for this success. Case 1 reported below echoes, in part, these phenomena.

Case vignettes

I give below a sample of actual experiences with time-limited counselling which have been disguised to protect confidentiality.

Case 1

Arthur, a man in his late 50s, was experiencing serious problems at work. He was stressed, lacked concentration and found himself getting wound up and ready to get into fights with the least provocation. He was urged to try the staff counselling service, which offered a maximum six sessions at any one time. Arthur had not used counselling before, was a working class man and did not read about matters psychological. Nevertheless he was more than ready to tell his story.

About 15 years before he had discovered that his wife, with whom he had been having many arguments about money, had had an affair and soon after this they parted. Not long after that, his mother died. Not knowing how best to cope with his troubled emotions, Arthur took a job in another part of the country, hoping to put everything behind him. For a while this seemed to work. Then he had to change his job. Gradually, after some years, he found himself in a working environment in which he felt extremely tense; he was getting older and younger men were promoted over him, or didn't take the job as seriously as he did. Things began to go very wrong and he couldn't see why.

Arthur met a woman who encouraged him to make the most of the free counselling available to him. He spent most of his first session in counselling pouring out the losses and frustrations of many years' standing. He and his counsellor briefly discussed assertiveness and relaxation techniques as an aid to his progress. Arthur did not envisage coming for regular or frequent counselling sessions and, indeed, did not return for another month. When he did, however, he seemed transformed. He had constructively lost weight, felt much less tense, was naturally acting more assertively at work and thereby earning respect, and, as an unexpected bonus, his eyesight had improved considerably. He attributed much of this to his one session of counselling.

The counsellor, tempted though he was to take the credit for this transformation, realised that Arthur had been very highly motivated and that, after many years of bottling up his sense of loss, anger, injustice and frustration, had mainly needed to talk cathartically and to be respected and encouraged. Although no formal follow-up or evaluation was conducted, the counsellor heard fortuitously some 18 months later that Arthur was doing very well at work, had retained his gains and remained grateful for the counselling he had had. It would have been tempting for some therapists strongly to encourage Arthur to remain 'in therapy' in order to examine and work through his presumed low self-esteem, fragile ego, placatory tendencies, and so on. The reasons for his original choice of wife in relation to his relationship with his mother could have been investigated; indeed all sorts of hypotheses could have been generated and worked on. But what worked for Arthur was the timely expression of a great deal of suppressed feeling, followed by experiencing himself differently, valuing himself and consistently behaving differently. More sessions of counselling could even have undermined his progress.

Case 2

Christina, an office worker of 28, saw a counsellor in connection with the death of her father. The first anniversary of his death was approaching and she had not, she believed, come to terms with the loss. The first session was spent discussing the circumstances of his death, Christina's feeling about him, how she was coping on a day-to-day basis, and her hopes of counselling.

At the second session, Christina revealed that although she was indeed still upset about her father's death, she had a much more pressing matter to deal with, which turned out to be a compulsive problem. She described her ritual of checking locks, taps and electrical appliances within the house and of having an overly conscientious nature generally. The counsellor, Jackie, was somewhat thrown by this for three reasons. First, she had anticipated further bereavement work, with which she would have felt fairly comfortable. Secondly, she had only limited experience of working with obsessive and compulsive problems. Thirdly, within her agency's policies she could offer the client only eight sessions and she doubted if this was sufficient in a case like Christina's. She certainly considered trying to refer Christina on, but Christina preferred to continue working with Jackie 'at least to give it a try' and also because 'it was so hard getting myself here, I don't know if I could start all over again with someone else'.

A fairly detailed description of Christina's habits was elicited. She would mainly be preoccupied with her rituals in the evening, finding it hard to go to bed unless she had unplugged and checked all sockets, double-locked the front door, and so on. She would always check several times that she had locked the doors of her car. She knew that she over-tightened taps. She knew that her actions were unnecessary and irrational and she wanted to abandon them. Her father had had very similar traits. An investigation of possible causes of the condition did not seem fruitful since Christina could only report that she had 'always been like it, for as long as I can remember'. There were no obvious traumatic or causative events.

Christina was very clear that only eight sessions were being offered and she accepted this. Jackie felt that, on the plus side, Christina was highly motivated, there was a good alliance between them and Christina might not readily give it a second try if she had to start with another therapist. Jackie herself felt very motivated and believed that is was realistic to hope for at least some significant improvement, if not complete removal of symptoms. She was realistic enough to put aside – or at least to attempt no more than occasional – psychodynamic interpretations, both because she was familiar with some of the behavioural literature on obsessive–compulsive disorders and because she realised that Christina's orientation was towards a thinking and doing, problem-solving approach.

Working with a roughly agreed hierarchy of troublesome behaviours, Christina set herself first to prevent herself from checking the locks of her car. This she managed to achieve quite

*rapidly. She wasn't wholly free of the compulsion to check them,
but largely so. She maintained and marginally improved this for
the next two or three weeks, using in-session time for reporting on
progress, setbacks, and exploration of any subtle factors involved.
Next she attempted to leave the taps alone after the first tightening.
This was harder, creating more mental anguish, but some
progress was made. Session by session, maintenance of gains was
discussed and reference was made regularly to the number of
sessions used and still available. Christina herself suggested that
the remaining sessions be staggered.*

Case 3

*Michael began counselling following the break up of his marriage
of 12 years. He had three children who he missed a great deal. He
was still very fond of his wife and still saw her but was quite
certain the marriage was over. He blamed himself; he'd buried
himself in his work – he was a computer specialist, indeed he was
fanatical about computers, spending most of his spare time
attending computer fairs, conferences, and so on. He fully agreed
that during his marriage, and probably for a long time before, he
had been cut off from his feelings. He wasn't surprised his wife
had ended the marriage, he just wished he had seen it coming
and still had time to change things.*

*He often cried in the sessions. He spontaneously talked about
his past, about his relatively unfeeling parents, and his tendency
from an early age to immerse himself in books, in making things
and in sport. He had always been quite shy and awkward
around people. He liked them but didn't know how to initiate
conversation. When he met his wife, he knew how much the
attraction was due to her freedom of expression, her comfort with
anger and messy emotions. They had been deeply in love,
obviously getting something compensatory from each other. With
the passing of the years, the children growing up and his wife
becoming angry with her taken-for-granted role, things were
bound to have to change significantly. Yet Michael immersed
himself more and more in his work and interests, thus effectively
cutting himself off altogether from his wife.*

*Counselling with Michael proceeded meanderingly. By nature
(or misfortune) a highly methodical person, the last thing he now
needed was an overly methodical approach to counselling. The*

counsellor sensed that this was the case and allowed – indeed encouraged – Michael to wander over many areas of his current and past life, sometimes achieving a little insight, sometimes simply needing to cry and grieve. Michael's statutory eight sessions seemed to be used up rapidly. What he had gained was a taste for looking inward and dwelling on feelings, wishes and disappointments. A lifetime of somewhat obsessional, unsociable behaviour cannot perhaps be overturned overnight. Michael asked for advice on how he could continue with this new found taste for talking about feelings and exploring relationships, and the counsellor put him in touch with a therapeutic group.

Case 4

Gwen was referred to a counsellor following the dramatic termination of a cult-like organisation in which she had been involved. A third party was footing the bill and sessions were limited to 10. The first session was spent partly on exploring Gwen's experiences of being involved in the organisation and on eliciting her specific needs in counselling. It emerged that what was most devastating for her were feelings not of abuse but of loss. She had lost a structure and to some extent a group of friends; but furthermore, probing revealed that much of her life had been devoted to searching for some kind of security. Her father had died when she was a child and she had grown up with a vague but constant sense of something missing. The counsellor took the risk of focusing very sharply on this loss. Officially the brief of the referring agency was that the counsellor should debrief the client for a kind of post-cultic trauma. This was not, however, what the client presented. Everything pointed to unresolved early loss and the emotional, somatic and behavioural consequences flowing from it.

By the fourth and fifth sessions Gwen had gained access to harrowing feelings of grief. Upon allowing herself to cry more than ever previously, she found herself temporarily feeling worse and being inclined to be less sociable. The counsellor encouraged her to remain in touch with these changes while at the same time looking forward to how she might order her behaviour differently. For example, it had been her habit to work very diligently, to play hard and to vigorously pursue friends and partners. On reflection, she decided that it might be better to spend some more time alone, not running away from her inner pain; also, she learned to discriminate between angry and sad feelings, and came to identify and own the latter more. Although the process was painful, Gwen agreed that it had to be engaged in. The counsellor felt some concern at the shortage of time allotted and checked at intervals with Gwen to ascertain whether she felt secure enough to aim to terminate within the specified time. Another consideration in this case was that Gwen had demonstrated some previous tendency towards injudicious dependency, so the counsellor did not wish to repeat the pattern.

Gwen went through a period of intense feelings, often anger at her mother and others in her life. This was not forced by the counsellor but emerged as a necessary process. Gwen herself requested that the sessions be staggered, allowing her to deal with some of her frightening feelings herself and to maximise the usefulness of the 10 sessions. At the ninth session she reported that things had changed a great deal for her; although still experiencing intense feelings, these were now understandable, manageable and productive. She had definitely turned a corner in her life. She decided that it was not necessary to use the final session. The counsellor explicitly explored with Gwen the possibility of this being a 'flight into health', but she did not consider it to be so. Together they agreed that the tenth session could be held in reserve for a follow-up or emergency if need be. It is worth noting that with or without discussion, some clients elect to terminate time-limited counselling one session before the final available session. In fact, Gwen made contact some months later because she was feeling desolate. This feeling related to a sense of social rejection, plus a cluster of sensations and feelings of loss, need and fear of driving people away. Within two further sessions, through insight, learning and acceptance of the roots of these feelings, Gwen had stabilised.

A summary of Gwen's case follows.

The case of Gwen

Presenting problem:	*'Cult' survivor*
Affect:	*Non-specific rage; fear of loss of control*
Behaviour:	*Needy yet sometimes self-isolating; occasional fast driving*

Disclosure:	*Father died when she was five years old*
Risk factors:	*Dependency on counsellor; loss of control*
Time factors:	*10 session limit (third party paying)*
Previous therapy:	*None*
Extratherapeutic factors:	*Friends, own home, career, religious faith*
Alliance:	*Fortuitous rapport with counsellor; some common interests and attitudes*
Working hypothesis:	*Unresolved, lifelong grief leading to seeking and anger*
Therapeutic process:	*Encourage memory recall, catharsis, insight; homework (contact mother); convert rage to sadness*
Attendance pattern:	*Weekly, changing to fortnightly, then three-weekly; one session held in reserve*
Outcome:	*Significant insights and past–present connections; ability to grasp and manage critical rage–sadness flashpoint; realistic assessment of present circumstances and plans; realistic view of cult; improved family relations*
Retrospective assessment:	*Good alliance; seen promptly; life event turning point; highly motivated and insightful*
Relapse risks:	*Depression; further rejection/loss experiences*
Prognosis:	*Stable improvement*
Follow-up:	*The client made contact some months later; she had indeed experienced some rejection and isolation and felt devastated. Two further sessions helped her to consolidate her gains*

Case 5

Hannah used her student counselling service to talk about why she felt so stressed. She was a final year student and on the face of

*it her problems might stem from academic pressure and future
insecurity. But Hannah gave examples of losing her temper and
driving herself hard in other areas of her life that suggested she
was trying to conceal something. No examples of early life crises
or traumas could be discovered, however; there was no obvious
sibling rivalry or other factors which might have helped explain
why she now drove herself so hard. The counsellor persisted quite
hard within the first and only session to find a focus for
Hannah's stress.*

*Sometimes clues present themselves in what clients are refusing
to discuss or what they mention in a throwaway manner.
Hannah began to describe an angry scene she had had with a
girlfriend but then abandoned her tale and went on to talk about
something else. When she could, the counsellor encouraged her to
return to the angry scene. Applying a certain pressure, she
benignly cornered Hannah emotionally until Hannah told the
full story of this incident. As the counsellor persisted and
identified a theme of 'I have to remain tough always', Hannah
showed visible signs of wanting to cry. As she allowed herself to
cry, the counsellor suggested that perhaps her stress derived, at
least in part, from the lifelong strain of trying to maintain a
tough facade instead of letting herself admit to having a
vulnerable side. The counsellor did not insist to Hannah that she
should cry or that she should accept this interpretation, indeed
she suggested several other possible interpretations and strategies
for dealing with stress. It was, however, clear that therapeutic gold
had been struck, since Hannah herself began to insist through
her tears that this insight was exactly right for her.*

*It was possible for the counsellor to zoom in in this way because
she was experienced, flexible and confident. Had Hannah been
more receptive to discussing relaxation strategies, the counsellor
would have pursued those. Had there seemed to be historical clues
to abuse or early hurts, she would have followed those. But she
identified a vein of suppressed emotion accompanied by a
counterproductive self-image. She did not judge the client to be
essentially fragile. She picked up on a contradiction between the
client's physical strength and initial 'let's get down to business'
manner on the one hand, and minor avoidances and glints of
unguarded feeling on the other. The counsellor liked Hannah but
had no investment in talking her into lengthy therapy. Now,
Hannah was not exactly a case of crisis intervention but she had*

reached a critical point and the counsellor's hunch was to utilise this. At the end of this first session Hannah said that she had a quite different perspective on her stress and could see what she could do to alleviate it. Talking about it in counselling would not be the agent of change. She was assured that she could return at any time but she showed no sign that she felt a need to.

Each of the above cases (Cases 1–5) represents degrees of success, from the apparently miraculous to the modest initiation into further therapy elsewhere. I turn now to some examples of rather less successful short-term or time-limited counselling (Cases 6–8). This is partly to acknowledge that, like any counselling, time-limited counselling is not a panacea and sometimes goes wrong. But it is also partly because we have much to learn from failure.

Case 6

Brian, a man in his mid-20s, sought counselling from a voluntary agency because he was experiencing acute shyness and social anxiety. Although the agency did not strictly limit the number of sessions, there was an expectation that most work would be brief, and counsellors had to present a very strong case to their manager for extending the work beyond 12 sessions. Brian had tried counselling before on two separate occasions without success, once with someone who used a variety of behavioural and hypnotherapeutic methods and once with someone working generically. The current counsellor, Sheila, practised eclectically following an initial training in psychodynamic counselling. Brian had had an assessment session and seemed well motivated, which was one of the agency's criteria for acceptance.

Brian reported that for the past 10 years he had suffered from anxiety feelings related to social situations. He had felt forced to avoid certain encounters at school, college and in his present job. He avoided any situation requiring a public or semi-public performance of any kind; he usually avoided parties and other gatherings, even when he knew most of the people; he sometimes avoided friends and hid at home. When Brian had accidentally found himself in any challenging social situation, he usually 'kicked himself' mentally afterwards for, as he believed, saying all the wrong things or failing to come up with interesting or relevant things to say. Blushing, dizziness and palpitations were some of the symptoms he typically experienced. His working class family had been fairly retiring and he perceived his problems as stemming at least in part from finding himself, since secondary school days, with more middle class people. He had a degree and a modest professional job but was not doing particularly well.

Sheila's hunch was that with some sensitive encouragement towards doing pertinent homework assignments (exposing himself gradually to anxiety-inducing situations and keeping a diary of typical thoughts, feelings and avoidant patterns), Brian might make reasonably rapid progress. Brian agreed to try these assignments. However, by the fifth session he was obviously not doing well. He reported that he had tried to force himself to talk to people and to speak up in an evening class; this had resulted in feeling worse and he had stopped attending the class altogether. He became demoralised and Sheila assured him that he was not obliged to maintain the homework. Unfortunately, given his previous 'failed' therapies and his already very low self-esteem, Brian now used this lack of progress to confirm his worst fears: he would never improve.

Sheila discussed this work in supervision, agreed that certain countertransference phenomena were evident (she now also felt she was failing) and began to change tack. Further exploration of Brian's past was instigated and he did indeed recall some significant memories. However, session 10 had now been reached and there was no prospect at all that he would overcome his anxiety within 12 or even several additional sessions. Both Sheila and Brian were convinced that open-ended counselling was necessary. Sheila's manager did not support this idea (the waiting list was growing and Brian's problem was by no means the most serious) and she made some unsuccessful attempts to find somewhere she could refer him to for long-term counselling or therapy. Since he had little disposable income and probably felt by now pretty demoralised, he told Sheila that she had helped all she could and he would do his best to get by. In fact he did not attend his last scheduled session and did not reply to Sheila's letter offering to reschedule it.

Discussion points
1   Should Brian have been assessed more carefully and not been taken on for short-term counselling at all?

2 Has this experience damaged him or set him back, or was it a worthwhile experience?
3 Would it have been better if Sheila had worked in a consistently psychodynamic way from the outset?
4 Should Sheila have fought harder with her manager to keep seeing Brian for much longer?
5 What ethical issues may be involved in this case?

Case 7

Sharon worked in a factory and had recently witnessed a fatal accident involving a workmate. A piece of machinery had, in a freak incident, come loose at the worst possible moment and caused instantaneous death to a worker. Sharon was sent home and later referred to the company's employee assistance programme (EAP). She went to see Dave, who worked as an affiliate of the EAP from his own consulting room at home. Dave had had a few encounters with survivors of traumatic incidents and his supportive, relationship-based style of counselling seemed to have achieved moderate success.

Sharon had not had counselling before, did not know what it entailed and did not feel very positively about it. She wanted to forget about the incident as quickly as possible, and she could not understand what Dave was trying to achieve when he constantly repeated what she said and did not provide her with any new ideas for coping with her problems. She did not find his room or his informal manner inspiring, having expected to see someone like a medical expert – perhaps a hypnotherapist who could 'make it all go away'. After two sessions of a maximum possible six, Sharon failed to return. Dave heard some time later that she had been referred to an occupational psychologist who had in fact employed some kind of hypnotic technique with success.

Discussion points
1 Is it possible to help every client with one counselling approach?
2 Is it realistic to 'send' clients with no previous knowledge about counselling to a counsellor working in private practice?
3 Is there an optimal time following a traumatic incident for someone to attend for counselling?

4 Could Dave have acted differently, even within his preferred
   theoretical orientation, to increase the chances of Sharon continuing to come for counselling?
5 Should Dave have immediately referred Sharon to a practitioner specialising in helping people suffering from post-
   traumatic stress?

Case 8

*Bob was a serving police officer at the time of the Hillsborough
Disaster in 1989. He was directly involved in trying to control
and redirect the panicking crowd. It took a while for him to
realise that people had already died. One particular red-headed
young man was obviously dead. Bob himself fell at one point and
almost sank to his own death. Some spectators were still
complaining that they could not see the game. Police officers
were trying to resuscitate people. Bob, for the sake of safety, had to
hold a gate closed to the enclosure, even when a father asked to
look for his 12-year-old son. Bob had the task of collecting
discarded personal possessions from the scene, during which he
stopped someone from pocketing wallets and valuables. It hit him
hard when he discovered, and then saw for himself, that at least
92 bodies had been recovered. After the incident he felt so
disgusted and disoriented that he had his uniform burnt. He
returned to work and tried to put the whole incident behind him.
A mass critical incident debriefing was organised but Bob
declined to attend. Some officers went sick and never returned;
some had breakdowns. Bob himself carried on at work somehow
for about two years, although at home he was extremely
impatient and difficult, and his physical health was very bad. He
had somehow dissociated from the event, but his body and
behaviour betrayed his distress. Fear of dismissal from his job
added to Bob's tendency to hide the extent of his continuing
distress.*

*Bob had access to an occupational psychologist but delayed
making contact until he almost broke down. The psychologist
analysed his breathing (he was hyperventilating) and prescribed
bed rest for three weeks. He gave him permission to be ill, which
indeed he was. This acknowledgement helped considerably. Bob
started to pretend, however, that he now felt better than he really
did. Soon he broke down again and finally accepted retirement*

on the grounds of ill health. He was offered eye movement desensitisation and reprocessing (EMDR), a technique aimed at bringing his intrusive traumatic images under control. He had three or four sessions of this. Even after the first session, he felt a great deal of relief after confronting the painful images repeatedly. However, his sensitivity to these images returned within about two weeks. Bob later attributed the helpfulness of these meetings mainly to being told that his problems were physical and that he was ill. Later, medication intended to address his serotonin deficiency also helped. Gradually Bob restored some normality to his life and, in retrospect, is unsure how much permission to be ill, medication, EMDR or his own strength saved him. Nothing, according to Bob, can prepare anyone for a trauma like Hillsborough. He had experienced many violent incidents, deaths and gory scenes before that. Somehow he survived Hillsborough, although not without having to give up his job and change his priorities.

In Bob's case EMDR did not offer the dramatic salvation reported by McCann (1992). Why? Did the enormity of the event make it impossible for him to overcome understandable distress? Did the EMDR help somewhat? Bob said at the time that it was 'very useful', indeed 'fabulous', but it gave only short-lived relief. To this day Bob avoids crowds. His life has changed altogether and in some ways is better: 30 years of macho behaviour as a policeman has given way to a softer, more vulnerable, perhaps more human way of being. 'It's OK to be ill', says Bob. This is one of his major lessons. It may be that therapeutic techniques designed rapidly to banish distress overlook the realities and needs of the body. It may be that certain techniques work well fortuitously for some, but not for others. Bob wonders whether suggestibility was part of the modest success of the EMDR in his case, since it was presented as a promising new technique.

Discussion points
1 Is it likely that short-term behavioural or similar treatments following major disasters will be successful?
2 To what extent can success and failure in short-term therapy be attributed to clients' individual differences?
3 To what extent can various therapeutic inputs (EMDR, medication, rest, self-help, family support) be separated when trying to understand how people are helped?

4 Does Bob's case suggest that a multimodal assessment (Lazarus, 1989) might indicate that trying to help him initially via a medical/physical route would have held the best promise for success?

Sample of counsellor statements in sessions of time-limited counselling

Let us now turn out attention briefly to some of the micro aspects of time-limited counselling. What do counsellors find themselves actually saying and doing within sessions where time is of the essence?

Opening statements
Compare the following statements.

> As you know, we have 10 sessions of 1 hour available. From the literature we sent you, you will know that this is a confidential service. You've said that you want to discuss your tendency to get rather depressed. Would you like to begin with that right away, or is there anything you'd like to ask me first?

This somewhat brisk beginning reminds the client that time is limited but also invites him or her to launch into his or her story. Although the counsellor's intention is to focus on depression, the counsellor gives the client some opportunity to raise anything else that may be significant.

> I see from the questionnaire you completed for us that you've lived with this problem for quite a while. Well, I'm pretty sure you'll be glad to get rid of it and I'm very keen to help you.

Here, the counsellor creates expectancy. Without waiting for the client to spell things out, the counsellor goes directly from pre-counselling information to therapeutic activity. Here the attempt is to elicit the client's motivation to overcome the problem and for the counsellor to convey his or her own enthusiasm and commitment.

> Let's use this first session to get to know each other. Also, I'd like to know as much about what's on your mind as possible. Next time we meet we'll try to focus down on some specifics, but for now please say whatever's on your mind.

This counsellor takes control (not of the client but of the process) and offers an immediate structure. The client may feel free to talk about anything; indeed the task for him or her is to do just this. The counsellor has both set a constructive agenda for the next session and set the tone for an active approach.

Which kind of opening statement sounds most welcoming and effective to you?

Crunch points

Obviously there are many potentially difficult moments in any therapy. Two typical crunch points in time-limited counselling are worth looking at. The first is the common experience of the wandering client, the person who either does not know how or who is too anxious to focus their conversation on meaningful personal material, and who rambles incessantly or periodically. In very short-term counselling it is not possible simply to 'go with' this and see what happens. Development of the skills of interruption is essential! How do you interrupt firmly and constructively? First, you are less likely to encounter this problem if you have previously explained the nature of time-limited counselling and the need to focus. Secondly, if you have previously given some explanation and formulated a contract, you have a licence to interrupt, perhaps with: 'You remember that we agreed to avoid talking around things and to focus on the really important matters . . .'. Thirdly, if you have not previously explained the need for a focus or your client continues to ramble, you may have to suggest a little 'time out'. It might take this form:

> If I may, I'd like us just to step back for a few minutes. I appreciate that you have a lot to say but our time is relatively short and I want to make the best use of it to help you overcome your anxiety. Can we come back to what you first said about when and where you get most anxious?

This is firm, polite enough and should achieve successful interruption. There is no need to begin analysing the client's need to ramble (unless it is strictly related to their presenting concern).

The second common crunch point is observed in client statements to the effect that the 6 or 12 sessions may not be enough after all. 'I really don't know if I can do this. Twelve sessions is an awfully short time considering the life I've had', or 'But my friend is in therapy, he's been going for three years and he says there's no way anything can be done in a few weeks', are examples of the types of statement you may hear. Sometimes these are reasonable doubts but sometimes they are defensive manoeuvres. In any case, how likely are you – as the counsellor – to concede? If you know that the client simply has no access to alternative, long-term services, you might sympathetically agree that the time is short but better than nothing. If you suspect that the client is playing some sort of game, you might paradoxically agree that change cannot be achieved in this short time and the client should seek out the longest possible contract with a private practitioner. More commonly, you may need to say something like:

> It's a short time, certainly, but you agreed to it; I think you could see that real progress is possible, and I assure you that many people have benefited from the time-limited therapy here. It can sometimes feel very challenging, even frightening, but perseverance usually pays off. Shall we continue where we left off?

When challenged in these ways you must obviously be reasonably convinced yourself that it is right to counter-challenge the client. You need to do so in a way that is congenial. You may sometimes use the client's wariness to their advantage (for example, 'The fear you're expressing is a sign that we're touching on something important'), or occasionally you may need to reconsider whether a short-term approach is right for them.

Closing statements
Compare the following statements.

> As you know, this is the fifth session and only one session remains. We seem to have covered many of the concerns you spoke about when you first came here. Is that your view?

The counsellor does not avoid raising the subject of the finiteness of the counselling contract, he or she volunteers a personal view of what has been achieved and then invites the client to comment.

> I think you've made considerable progress in these six sessions and there are now two left. Are there any particular concerns left that you'd like to discuss; or would you like to review what we've done together?

This statement reinforces the client's progress and presents him or her with an opportunity to consider how to use the remaining two sessions. There is still time to look at something new, or the time could be used to return to certain themes and strengthen progress.

This is our last session, as you know. Speaking for myself, I've been really impressed at how much you've changed. But I also want to say that I've learned a lot from you and I've felt close to you. I'll miss you.

Counsellors often find endings with clients difficult or emotional and face decisions about whether they will, as a result, fudge the ending or disclose their real feelings. This statement shows firmness about this being the final session; the counsellor acknowledges the client's progress but also discloses his or her own feelings. This is a personal risk for the counsellor and it may be hard for the client to take. Alternatively, it may offer permission to reciprocate and may signal a return to 'normality'.

What do you think are the advantages and disadvantages of each of the above statements?

Sample of tasks across sessions

Certain approaches to time-limited therapy require fairly methodical coverage of tasks. This is true of cognitive analytic therapy (Ryle, 1990, 1995) and contextual modular therapy (Macnab, 1993). Brief computer-assisted therapy is structured around fixed sessions and graded tasks. Task completion is also characteristic of implicitly brief approaches where no precise end point is set (Egan, 1994; Dryden and Feltham, 1992). Here I outline a possible sequence of counsellor-initiated tasks across sessions in an illustrative time-limited therapy of six sessions.

Session 1
Greeting (warm, deliberate); engendering hope, interest and commitment; establishing therapeutic bonds; inviting the client to talk and set the scene; encouraging catharsis; contracting at a suitable level; listening for a focus; trial mini-therapy if indicated; establishing whether one session is sufficient, whether referral is indicated, or continuation; identification of goals and homework likely to facilitate desired direction; hand out any useful literature, questionnaires, etc.; warm farewell.

Session 2
Greeting; making space for any comments in general, plus feedback on progress or reflections on experiences since last meeting; checking on success of any homework suggested; establishing

focus for this session; agreeing on usefulness of particular therapeutic tasks; launching into active therapy mode; observation of
impact; inviting feedback from client; reviewing what has been
learned or uncovered, what has been useful, etc.; homework for
ensuing week; reminder of time limits; farewell.

Session 3

Greeting; space for comments; encouraging client to set agenda
and report on the week's experiences, including homework;
reflections on therapeutic progress so far, inviting client to suggest
changes; agree on focus; rapid entry into therapeutic work;
increase level of challenge; push for more relevant details of
history, core conflicts, problematic relationships, desired changes,
identifiable self-sabotaging strategies; convey sense of mid-way
tension; homework; farewell.

Session 4

Greeting; space for comments/feedback; convey sense of time
passing; identify elements of progress, resistance, remaining goals;
examine possibility of dealing with major or overarching themes,
life hopes, regrets, etc.; push for major cognitive or affective
problem areas; work on session focus; feedback; review best use
of therapeutic time, decide on staggered further sessions if felt
advisable; discuss risk–stasis balance sheet non-judgementally;
agree on contract; farewell.

Session 5

Greeting; space for comments and progress review; celebration of
any successes; analysis of any failures; focus on work for session;
raise issues of relapse and suggest possible strategies; openly
discuss this as penultimate session and invite real feelings about
ending; invite client to raise any new material to work on ('we still
have time'); agree on arrangements for last session; farewell.

Session 6

Greeting; space for comments; review progress of counselling;
offer time for final, possibly quite deep therapeutic focus; invite
client to summarise major gains, disappointments, understanding
of strengths, defences, remaining goals and fears; give full feedback to client, possibly also written report or goodbye letter; agree
on whether this is final or an extended contract, follow-up or

open door is on offer; disclose any helpful personal reactions to ending with the client; warm farewell.

There is no ideal blueprint of how sessions will progress, models such as Macnab's (1993) notwithstanding. The above is a suggestion of some of the points likely to arise or which require attention. Exactly how six sessions are used will depend on your personal orientation and style, and on the client's readiness, problems and personality. What can be said with some confidence is that a structure must be held in mind; some sort of contracting must be engaged in; and decisions about foci, and the depth and kind of therapeutic work indicated, are needed.

7

Problems and Troubleshooting

In this chapter I look at some common problems and obstacles encountered by those working in a time-limited way. To some extent, some of them have already arisen or have been anticipated earlier. Where possible I have included suggestions for dealing with particular problems. Practitioners who use ostensibly watertight assessment procedures, excluding clients who pose any risk to therapeutic success, try to do all their troubleshooting at the outset! I suggest that problems will always occur. A traditional remedy has been to give interminable therapy and, in some cases, simply to increase the frequency of sessions. In some cases of time-limited counselling, however, the only remedy is preparation by training. Anticipating such problems and setbacks may in itself sensitise you to early signs of their appearance in practice.

Pre-set time limits just don't suit everyone

There is a very good case for saying that a pre-set limit to the number of sessions is arbitrary and likely to be a mismatch for at least some clients, in spite of Mann's (1973) insistence on firm time limits. How can we say that everyone will benefit equally from 6, 12 or 16 sessions, for example? Personalities, needs, and the idiosyncratic clusters in which people's problems are found surely mean that there should always be some flexibility about the number of sessions. Most first-time clients will have little or no idea of how counselling feels and will not be able to judge realistically whether a preordained number of sessions will be helpful. For some, the offer of eight hours to discuss anything about themselves seems like a luxury at the outset, but by the eighth session it may seem woefully inadequate. For others, the mention of eight sessions will mean: 'Am I really that sick?'. As Oldfield puts it:

> Some clients will feel, towards the end of the first session, which lasts fifty minutes, that they have only just begun to explain a long and complicated story; others, having succinctly summarised the trouble in the first few minutes, will already feel they have been there a long time, perhaps too long. (Oldfield, 1983: 16)

Educating clients into the role of an informed and active participant in short-term counselling does not guarantee that they will be able to use the prescribed time as expected. Even when good assessment procedures are followed there are no guarantees that a client will not break down after a few sessions and obviously need much longer. Even when the client presents with clear focal concerns and is well motivated at the outset, he or she may be unable to give up his or her compulsive rituals, for example. Now, if your assessment procedure is such that only clients with the most moderate and circumscribed problems are accepted, then you may indeed minimise difficulties like these. Lazarus and Fay (1990: 45) accuse the short-term dynamic therapist Sifneos of just such exclusive selection criteria. These authors incidentally argue that, in spite of their preference for brief and efficient therapy, a policy of an arbitrarily pre-set time limit is untenable. Bond (1993: 192) gives a specific example of how time-limited counselling could even present a serious ethical dilemma for counsellors.

Some people using easy-access counselling services which operate time-limited policies will be quite new to counselling. For some of them, the outcome may be the realisation that their concerns or problems are much deeper or more complex than they had thought. One of the functions of counsellors in such settings is often to help clients identify and accept this. It is not so unusual, for example, that in an EAP setting some clients will be advised by their counsellor to consider long-term therapy, if necessary taking on board the need to pay for it privately. Counsellors in this position need to look out for such clients at an early stage, perhaps suggesting to them in session three out of a possible eight sessions that they may well need to consider the longer-term option. However, such judgements obviously relate to counsellors' own views about the capacity of time-limited counselling (and their own skills) to address a variety of present-ing problems, as discussed in Chapter 4.

Dealing with crisis and relapse

The easy access nature of some counselling (for example, in EAPs, student services, and some voluntary and statutory agen-cies) means that some clients utilise them mainly in crises. Sometimes they may be used inappropriately, when the person could quite easily have coped alone or with normal support systems. But sometimes they are so readily available that life crises are taken automatically to the counsellor. This need not be problematic: sometimes a short supportive or catalytic session with a counsellor helps a client to get back on track.

There are, perhaps, basically four kinds of crisis problem in time-limited counselling. First, people often arrive for a first session immersed in their crisis (I've lost my job, my wife has left me, I've been diagnosed as having a critical illness, I've been mugged, I'm having panic attacks, etc.). This kind of presentation often externalises the problem (something has happened *out there*) and pushes the counsellor into a purely firefighting posi-tion. Perhaps the entire six sessions of a six-session contract may be used in dealing with the crisis. Secondly, some clients will present for counselling calmly, on some pretext, and find them-selves plunged into crisis as they begin to retrieve memories, realise the enormity of something that has happened to them, or sense terror as they begin to touch on extremely painful material. Halfway through an eight-session contract, what are they (and you) to do? Thirdly, occasionally chance events such as serious illness or accidents, bereavements and losing a job may occur within the duration of counselling. These may force the counsellor to consider whether to extend or modify the original contract. Fourthly, panic arises for certain clients due to the separation represented by the ending of counselling itself. Relapse is often just such a crisis, experienced when the clients realise they are about to be on their own and lose all confidence in their own coping abilities.

Develop a crisis detector which will alert you to these various expressions of crisis and panic. Decide whether you will offer crisis intervention to those clients who are essentially in a present crisis. Anticipate how you will deal with mid-contract clients who become panicky. Will you teach relaxation strategies or cognitive disputing; prepare a referral strategy of your own; negotiate an extendable contract? Dealing with termination crises is an integral part of short-term work. Clients can be warned to expect such feelings (which may have a paradoxical effect). The anxiety associated with endings can be usefully incorporated into the therapy using psychodynamic techniques (Davanloo, 1990; Molnos, 1995), rational emotive behaviour therapy (Dryden, 1995), or other approaches. It may be appropriate to link the ending of time-limited therapy with other endings, or to use the client's sense of crisis or fear of relapse as examples of irrational beliefs. Imagery may be employed, for example a picture of a terrifying dragon representing crisis; slaying the dragon and conducting a post-mortem on it may yield insight into the psychic components of the crisis. There are many techniques for anticipating relapse and rehearsing coping strategies (Lazarus, 1989; Dryden and Feltham, 1992; Miller and Rollnick, 1991; Macnab, 1993). It is advisable for time-limited counsellors to expect crisis and relapse rather than to be taken by surprise or interpret such phenomena as evidence of failure.

Some clients may wish and need to continue working with their time-limited counsellor

However clear it is made that your work with clients must remain short term (as it is made clear in many settings), some clients will not have foreseen what has emerged and how strongly they feel about the importance of their relationship with the counsellor. I have worked in an agency where extensions of time were not entertained and where counsellors were forbidden to continue working with clients elsewhere, for example in their own private practices. Although this policy was devised for good reasons, in certain instances it was evidently unhelpful to some clients.

The client may say 'Yes, I understand, that's fine,' when presented with a non-negotiable maximum number of sessions at the outset, but may begin to feel anxious – perhaps even resentful – as the end approaches. In many cases these feelings can be confronted and used therapeutically, as in the work of Mann (1973) and Ryle (1990, 1995), but no doubt many counsellors will have experienced dilemmas. I have certainly heard conscientious practitioners expressing concern about a minority of clients who would have been better served by flexible contracting (either extending the number of sessions or allowing the client to be seen in private practice). Solutions or partial solutions to this dilemma include effective assessment and referral mechanisms, extendable contracts (Elton Wilson, 1996), staggered endings (Dryden and Feltham, 1992), respecting individuals' professional discretion, and working with a model of time-limited counselling that explicitly utilises a non-negotiable end-point as part of its therapeutic rationale. It may also be significant that most counsellors I have surveyed on this issue believe that clients are rarely *harmed* in such circumstances; rather, flexibility would simply be better for some.

Short-term counselling may attract practitioners who have not resolved their own unconscious personality problems

People who have trained in such a way that their therapeutic encounters – both as clients and as counsellors – have been mainly short ones, may be unaware of and unable to identify problematic, unconscious material. Anyone who is strongly attracted to working in this brief milieu is bound to ask themselves why. The answer may simply be that they prefer to work efficiently, as no doubt Albert Ellis would argue. Some will honestly answer that they prefer to work with material presented in crisis form, or with clients who wish to address urgent matters, or in agencies offering realistic short-term help. Some may candidly admit that they dislike very long-term therapy. A problem may arise, however, when practitioners are involved in short-term, time-limited counselling for the wrong reasons. (One can also be involved in long-term therapy for wrong reasons.)

Robertiello and Schoenewolf (1987), in their interesting and original compilation of countertransference and counterresistance vignettes, present the following case.

A therapist who specialised in a progressive form of short-term therapy treated a woman patient with techniques which precluded the creation of dependency. He cut short silences, generated liveliness and eschewed confrontation. When the woman met and began a relationship with an older man, the therapist encouraged this and interpreted it as a signal that treatment was successful and complete. However, the woman went on to have a series of unsatisfactory relationships because, according to Robertiello and Schoenewolf, she was acting out and had acted out in response to the therapist's failure to address her unconscious manipulation of him. In this case, the authors argue that the therapist mistakenly regarded his work as successful and that this illustrates 'How a school of therapy can become a counterresistance' (1987: 249).

This is an interesting charge which we might learn from even if unconvinced by the authors' particular case example. It is, of course, quite possible that short-term counselling has developed and finds adherents due to unrecognised, unconscious resistance among practitioners. Counsellors unaware of or afraid of their own infantile material (for example, a need to experience lengthy intimacy and a degree of powerlessness in relationships), may gravitate towards short-term work to disguise this from themselves and others.

Like many similar arguments in the polemical field of counselling this one cannot be finally resolved; but counsellors and their trainers, therapists and supervisors would do well to keep in mind the potential for counterresistance and countertransference inherent in time-limited counselling. It would be superstitious to suggest that every short-term contract disguises unresolved unconscious material but, at initial assessment and as part of ongoing self-supervision, it is wise to consider how this work *might* at times mask issues more properly addressed in longer-term therapy.

Time-limited counselling may discourage clients from raising serious issues

Faced with access to a free, six-session counselling contract and having no other realistic options, most clients in need will proceed compliantly with it. The argument is sometimes put that they will, however, instinctively adapt themselves to present only material that feels manageable within a short time and may, therefore, be cheated of attention to their more serious problems or vulnerable feelings. In very brief therapy, perhaps, insufficient time is made available for establishing a trusting-enough relationship. In addition to this is the argument that clients in this position are likely to avoid challenging or upsetting their counsellors, for example by leaving negative reactions unspoken (Regan and Hill, 1992). Counsellors, too, may avoid voicing certain things within brief therapy for fear of opening up too many issues or feelings that may require lengthy therapy.

In this Regan and Hill study of six-session therapy it was found that certain significant, usually negative, thoughts and feelings were sometimes withheld by counsellors and clients. Regan and Hill speculate that 'perhaps clients have a defensive need to protect these vulnerable feelings in a brief therapy relationship' (1992: 173). They also question whether social proscriptions may account for clients withholding certain material. Reflecting on the probability that a majority of users of time-limited counselling may be people who cannot afford to pay for open-ended therapy – and therefore feel they must accept what they are offered – serious questions arise about the tendency of time-limited counselling to mute potentially time-consuming issues and feelings. This is an area where more research is clearly needed.

One way of addressing this is to consider extendable contracts. In one agency where six-session therapy is offered, some initial findings suggested that clients may be opting for closure by the fourth or fifth session rather than disclosing further important matters. A clear policy of allowing a further six sessions if needed appears to have lessened the tendency towards early closure (Peter Roberts, personal communication, 1996). In spite of this, the mean usage is still around three or four visits, which could reassure managers that flexibility of this kind does not necessarily open up the floodgates! Apart from such extensions, another strategy is to invite clients – either within or between sessions – to reflect on and disclose any sense of feelings or thoughts withheld; a purpose-designed mini-questionnaire might be given to elicit such possibilities.

Working multiculturally

I have previously alluded to the experience of Kottler (1993), who found attitudes towards punctuality in Peru very different from those he was accustomed to in the USA. Such impressions are formally confirmed by Sue and Sue (1990). They point out that there are widely differing temporal assumptions from culture to culture and that counsellors generally need to be aware of these in order to avoid errors stemming from their own temporal prejudices. Sue and Sue suggest that the dominant culture in US society is compulsive about time and is future-oriented; progress, the belief that time is money and that time should not be wasted are all strongly held values. By contrast, Native Americans and Black Americans are said to place more emphasis on present time, with Asian Americans and Hispanic Americans being more focused on the past–present. Sue and Sue argue that Puerto Ricans, for example, are much more likely to measure time by meaningful daily or periodic events than by rigid clock appointments. Clients who value a leisurely here and now focus may feel rushed and disrespected by a counsellor with a time-limited agenda. Discrepancies in culturally valued approaches to time generally can seriously hamper the therapeutic alliance. Sue and Sue further suggest that 'many minorities who overall are present-time oriented would be more likely to seek immediate, concrete solutions rather than future-oriented "abstract goals"' (1990: 128).

The same authors put the case, very succinctly, that for certain clients (for example, Native Americans and Hispanics) time-limited counselling may be highly problematic:

> Relative to White middle-class standards, deep friendships are developed only after prolonged contacts. Once friendships are formed, they tend to be lifelong in nature. In contrast, White Americans form relationships quickly, but the relationships do not necessarily persist over long periods of time. Counseling seems to also reflect these values. Clients talk about the most intimate aspects of their lives with a relative stranger once a week for a 50-minute session. To many culturally different people who stress friendship as a precondition to self-disclosure, the counseling process seems utterly inappropriate and absurd. After all, how is it possible to develop a friendship with brief contacts once a week? (Sue and Sue, 1990: 40)

These examples are taken from American literature. What is the case in Britain, which is also a multicultural community but has a different ethnic composition? First, some clues may be taken from class factors. Holmes and Lindley (1989) suggest that brief psychotherapy is more accessible to working class than to middle class patients because it is focused, goal-directed and clear in its guidance aspects. Ironically, as they point out, working class candidates are often not considered suitable for brief therapy because they display a higher incidence of addictive behaviours and suicidal tendencies (factors considered by many psycho-dynamic practitioners to militate against suitability for brief therapy), while middle class patients are likely to articulate their mental health needs better and to receive treatment earlier. The points made in the above section should also be considered: users of time-limited counselling services are likely to be on low to moderate incomes and to have little choice of treatment.

A project at the Women's Therapy Centre in London between 1990 and 1992, the Brief Psychotherapy Project, aimed to assess how useful time-limited therapy (up to 10 sessions) would be for certain groups prioritised according to need. These were black and Asian women, women from other ethnic minority commu-nities, Irish women, working class women on low incomes, lesbians and women with disabilities. Of those using this service, 65 per cent were on benefits and the rest on low incomes, 40 per cent had left school at 16 or earlier, 33 per cent suffered from depression, 75 per cent of the mothers were single parents, and 45 per cent were black women. In addition, 25 per cent had suffered childhood sexual abuse. Also ranking prominently were alcoholic backgrounds, histories of violence, dislocation from country of origin and other factors rendering these clients extremely vulnerable. Many of these women responded very well to time-limited therapy precisely because its finiteness did not overwhelm them. A majority gained real benefits from the therapy – essentially an integration of cognitive analytic therapy and psychodynamic therapy based on the work of Davanloo – as revealed in a one-year follow-up group (Mohamed and Smith, 1996).

When considering cultural differences we also perhaps need to bear in mind that one of the values of the therapeutic hour to clients, and to women in particular, is that it is protected time. It may be necessary, especially when approaching termination of time-limited counselling, to urge clients to maintain personally protected time. In Jocelyn Chaplin's words:

> For many clients their weekly sessions are the only regular times in their lives that are solely devoted to themselves. Feminist counsellors are particularly concerned that their clients find regular times, just for themselves, during the week. It may be possible to put aside time to write a diary every day, or meditate or just be still and with oneself. It is often very difficult for people in our culture just to *be*; they feel that they should always be *doing* something. (1988: 115)

Switching from short-term to long-term work

The reality for many practitioners is that they may work in different settings and within different policies. It is not unusual, for example, to work part-time in an agency and part-time in private practice. It may be that your agency operates a time-limited policy but that in your own practice you prefer open-ended or long-term work. (In fact this is highly likely.) I infer from my own experience that switching between such settings and their different demands may present problems.

Working in time-limited mode sensitises you to certain foci, goals and prohibitions. Almost inevitably, you become accustomed to swift assessment, readiness to refer when necessary, swift identification of patterns of problematic behaviour, rapid goal-setting, and a high level of challenge. You certainly become accustomed to endings! But in private practice (or indeed in any agency that has not introduced time limits) it is unlikely that you will contract with clients in the same way. It is sometimes the case that you are in one setting an hour or so after another setting, with a client who has no time limits to face. The difficulty here is in turning off the time-sensitised practitioner and becoming the open-ended practitioner, if this is called for. Without some way of regulating yourself in these circumstances, the danger is that you will inadvertently relate to your time-unlimited clients inappropriately. Hunter (1994) is in favour of time-limited counselling for women dealing with anxiety in pregnancy or facing issues prior to surgery, but cautions against it for those experiencing grief following a still-birth. Practice with variable temporal contracts (Elton Wilson, 1996) is obviously a useful way of learning to switch modalities positively and consciously.

Addressing the fantasy of instant cure and panacea

Time-limited counselling encourages an active, hopeful, forward-looking attitude. This can inadvertently create fantasies – perhaps in both counsellors and clients – of instant, dramatic cures or solutions. Certainly some of the brief therapy literature paints a picture of brilliant clinicians delivering exactly the right intervention at exactly the right moment to a well-motivated client whose life is changed overnight. In some cases the picture may be accurate but I suspect that most brief therapy, like most long-term therapy, is more often modest in its successes. Counsellors as well as clients should, preferably, consider their fantasies in advance.

Is it possible to distinguish between activity, hopefulness and a forward-looking attitude on the one hand, and a counterproductive therapeutic mirage on the other hand? A paradox is involved here. Disappointment is frequently, almost inevitably, a feature of most therapy. Life does not deliver to us everything that we want; likewise, counselling and therapy cannot deliver compensation for all our past suffering. We may never become perfectly assertive, relaxed, insightful, fearless, attractive, and so on. Somehow it is necessary within the parameters of brief time-limited counselling to convey the message that its gains usually cannot match any fantasies. This is recognised by Mann (1973), Garfield (1989), Ryle (1990) and Macnab (1993), among others.

Some of the ways in which fantasy can be doused include a statement in your literature to the effect that it is not magic, not a panacea; a verbal declaration by yourself at the outset; a question as part of your assessment which is designed to raise any unrealistic expectations; disappointment checks as part of review sessions; and acknowledgement of disappointments in goodbye letters (Ryle, 1990).

On being a slow learner or worker

While certain clients take a great deal of time because they are depressed, fearful or defensive, some take time simply because that is their style. Some of us talk and think slowly in comparison with others, who appear congenitally fast talkers and rapid decision makers. If any two clients were given single-session therapy and these sessions were transcribed and analysed, the likelihood is that they would not be working at the same pace. The same is true for counsellors too, of course. If you have watched Carl Rogers on video with a client like Gloria or Kathy, and you have also watched Albert Ellis or Arnold Lazarus, enormous differences are apparent. It is quite conceivable that some practitioners may cover twice as much ground as others. This is not necessarily *better* but it does raise clearly the problem of time limits.

In a client and counsellor dyad where both are fortuitously suited to thinking and working fast, a great deal may be achieved in three or four sessions. A much slower client–counsellor dyad might have difficulties within the same time frame. But even more problematic is the scenario where one party thinks and learns slowly while the other thinks and works fast. Given sufficient time to review such discrepancies together and to make adjustments, there need be no insurmountable problem (Dryden and Feltham, 1994: 53–6). However, if you work in a rigidly time-limited setting, careful thought should be given to potential problems of this kind. Indeed, ideally, training in short-term, time-limited counselling should take account of such factors. One way in which you can evaluate your own pace and how it might cause problems in short-term work is to tape-record some sessions, perhaps with the aid of a variety of colleagues, representing some slow and some fast learners and workers. Unfortunately, 'slow learner' often carries connotations of inferiority, which is unhelpful. If you suspect that either your client or you learn and work slowly (for non-psychopathological reasons!), then obviously this must be accommodated in some way. A variant of the slow learner problem is the client who rambles. Provided this is not defensive rambling, but a personality trait, the best you may be able to do is to remind the client how short and precious their time is. Again, training in relation to this problem would need to foster interruption and conversation management skills.

Breaking up is hard (for counsellors) to do

A significant problem for counsellors working in a short-term way was put to me by a psychodynamic counsellor who said that she found the relatively few clients she had to end with in long-term work emotionally draining, and therefore envisaged the necessarily greater number of endings in short-term work as being likely to be much more so. This impression is confirmed by Cummings (1990b: 173), Haley (1978) and Mann (1973). Perhaps for those counsellors or therapists who work in an emotionally intensive way, allowing themselves to get very close to and highly involved with clients, too many endings may prove too demanding. However, with due respect to these practitioners, I suggest the following counter-arguments.

First, as has been argued elsewhere in this book, a significant number of clients do not become long-term clients, whatever the original intention or contract was. Unless you manage to exclude brief clients and drop-outs altogether, most practitioners in fact experience a certain steady turnover. Secondly, brief therapy is clearly not experienced by all psychodynamic therapists as something to be avoided because it necessitates greater turnover and more endings to be dealt with (Molnos, 1995). Thirdly, those who work with a brief intermittent model, or episodically (Cummings, 1990b), perceive each of their clients as regularly coming and going, and therapy as being healthily interrupted rather than being terminated. Fourthly, a strong preference for open-ended work on the part of counsellors and therapists may conceal an unwillingness or apparent inability to confront separation, imperfection and disappointment. It may only be by engaging in both long-term and short-term work that practitioners can identify in themselves their own resistances to temporal boundaries.

Breaking up may indeed be very hard for counsellors as well as clients to do, but it may be a lesson that needs to be learned. If you realise that part of your resistance to time-limited work relates to your own history and personality (for example, you may have experienced particularly early or painful losses, your early life may have been characterised by too many house moves, or you may simply be phobic about endings and mortality), consider addressing this in therapy, in supervision, or existentially by facing just these situations.

8

Management of Time-
Limited Counselling in
Context

Since time-limited counselling is relatively new to the UK, issues relating to how it is to be managed are obviously quite new too. Yet all managers of counselling services have always been aware of funding constraints and the pressures of waiting lists, which both carry implications for the way in which counselling can be offered. Perhaps in certain NHS settings as well as in private practice, there has long been a vague expectation that much psychotherapy will be roughly limited, by the client's choice and/or speed of the therapeutic process, to about a year or two. But there has been little direct pressure, as far as I am aware, for service providers in the UK strictly to limit the number of sessions they offer. I suspect that this stems from the historical fact that a great deal of NHS and private practice psychotherapy is aligned with the ('timeless') psychoanalytic tradition. Many managers of counselling services are, of course, counsellors themselves; in addition, as senior practitioners, many will have been trained years ago, probably in the psychodynamic and person-centred traditions that had the field to themselves until recently. Things are, however, changing – both theoretically and economically. It seems almost inevitable that, to some extent at least, we will follow the American pattern (Cummings, 1988) of looking for accountability regarding time resources in British counselling and therapy services.

In this chapter a number of practice settings are briefly described, along with some of the management and clinical issues typically arising within them. Based on my own experience, I consider that actual and potential problems and significant issues for managers of such services include the following.

Employee assistance programmes

Employee assistance programmes (EAPs) have been among the first service providers to deal squarely with issues of managing time-limited work. EAPs operative within the UK include FOCUS, PPC, EAR, ICAS, Care Assist and Mentors Counselling Consultants. Some are based on American models but all practise time-limited work. I have encountered EAPs variously employing time limits of two, three, six, eight and ten sessions; in some cases these limits are negotiable. In some EAPs telephone counselling is provided with no time limits. These services are usually free to individual users, but in some cases employees requiring extra sessions have to pay for them.

In most cases the policy of short-term, time-limited work is directly linked with costings, since most run commercially and will obviously not finance open-ended counselling. But EAP providers are also aware: (a) that their credibility depends partly on seeing individual clients (users of their counselling services) promptly and dealing with them effectively, and (b) that both the clients and their employees are likely to perceive counselling as usually a short-term proposition. This latter perception also happens to correspond to some of the results of research. Time-limited counselling in an EAP setting, then, is likely to be managed pragmatically and efficiently. Yet even in these settings managers must sometimes make difficult decisions, such as those concerning assessment (should clients presenting with complex problems be referred elsewhere and, if so, where?) and termination (how does one handle those clients who, having used their quota of sessions, still need more?).

Usually the EAP guarantees to see clients promptly (for example, within two days, three days or a week), yet demand at any one time cannot be predicted; all service providers are aware of seasonal peaks and troughs of demand, as well as freak high demands, sometimes following a wave of publicity, a round of redundancies or a major traumatic event. Usually providers can rely on: (a) being able to call on one of their affiliated counsellors to see clients promptly, and (b) the fact that a significant number of clients will only come once or twice, and some will fail to turn up at all.

Even if a rigorous assessment procedure is in operation (and generally it probably is not, because within such short time limits an assessment session is itself time-consuming, plus assessment smacks of a clinical approach which many users would find stigmatising and off-putting), there are always clients whose 'real' problems become apparent only a few sessions into the thera-peutic process. In these cases it is of course essential that managers have policies and procedures in place: (a) to refer such clients on, if necessary by paying for at least some initial sessions or having an independent practitioner on retainer; and (b) to offer necessary flexibility to the EAP counsellor to continue working with such clients for a certain period.

The easy accessibility of EAPs can mean that people who otherwise would not have approached any mental health service, or would have found themselves on a long waiting list, may be seen immediately. More often than not this may work to the benefit of all concerned. Occasionally, however, clients may be seen who require psychiatric help, long-term psychotherapy or specialist services such as alcohol detoxification. With luck and/or excellent management, they should be referred promptly to appropriate sources of assistance but often there are no suitable resources available at all, or only after a long wait. These factors must be considered in advance. I am aware of at least one staff counselling service where excellent referral mechanisms are in place, but others often have a quite hit or miss approach or inadequate funding to offer, for example, to pay for the services of specialists.

EAP counselling which is very short-term and conducted within the organisation's premises or in similar office accommodation may not lend itself easily to powerful and emotive styles of humanistic or brief dynamic therapy. It is hard to imagine clients in such circumstances feeling safe and free enough to shout, cry deeply or engage in vigorous experiential or cathartic work. Where EAPs depend on annually renewable business contracts, an inhibiting factor may operate which prevents counsellors from undertaking particularly risky or challenging styles of counselling which could be perceived unfavourably by funders. It is worth noting in this context, too, that affect-laden work in particular generally challenges the ability of time limits (either within or across sessions) to contain and facilitate clients. Cunningham (1994: 131), however, considers that 'a typical use of short-term counseling involves non-pathological grief reactions in response to a loss.' Cunningham argues that most grief is time-limited and that prompt, short-term EAP counselling is appropriate in such cases. Worden (1991), however, argues that even simple grief may take some time, although actual client–counsellor contact need not necessarily be frequent.

Community and voluntary counselling agencies

Demand for the counselling and support services offered by Relate, MIND, Cruse, Victim Support and others continues to increase, irrespective whether or not additional funding is available. Local and regional, as well as specialist voluntary organisations, continue to grow. Some have grasped the nettle and introduced time-limited services (or other time-saving measures such as telephone and group counselling) but others have found themselves with growing waiting lists. Resistance to time-limited counselling is sometimes based on the religious foundations of charities and on the personal sentiments and theoretical orientations of counsellors. Where time limits have been introduced, this has not always been effected sensitively or wisely. I know one agency whose staff (mainly volunteer counsellors) were summarily ordered to begin limiting the number of sessions to six in every case. The counsellors were not consulted, nor were they offered training to help them do their work within these new parameters. They reported that the pressure on them was immense and they naturally floundered somewhat in the beginning when trying to explain these conditions to clients. Fortunately, there are other cases where agencies have sensitively and in consultation organised time-limited services (Grant et al., 1993).

Voluntary organisations often offer free or low-cost services and, therefore, attract those clients who may not be eligible for help elsewhere. The admirable humanitarian culture of such ventures unfortunately runs into frequent problems, however. Probably some of the most difficult-to-help clients, including those who have been rejected elsewhere, present for help to voluntary agencies. Typically, such agencies are staffed part-time by a mixture of paid and voluntary counsellors. Often training is in-house and supervision, too, is often supplied by the agency's own senior staff. Quite typically, counsellors have been trained in traditional models of psychodynamic, person-centred and three-stage (Egan, 1994) approaches, with only the latter having obvious time advantages.

More often than not, voluntary organisations focus on specific concerns such as relationship problems, bereavement, mental illness, HIV/AIDS, alcoholism and so on. Often counsellors in these settings have themselves recovered from similar problems. On the face of it, these narrowed focus and personal experience factors should make for very efficient services. Without challenging the excellent work that is done in such settings, it is apparent that it is not always as focused and efficient as it might be. Funding shortages may mean that counsellors do not receive the specialist training they need, for example. In addition, many counsellors find it hard – if not impossible – to remain focused on the presenting problems alone: clients who present with bereavement sometimes go on to disclose phobias, those with urgent HIV concerns may well wish to discuss other areas of their lives, drinking problems may be only the tip of an iceberg. Sometimes the solution may be to continue to work through all such issues, if the counsellor is competent to do so. Often referral is called for (yet there may be few or no alternative resources available). What could help immeasurably is training in assessment and counselling related to the further areas of need that are disclosed (Lazarus, 1987; Macnab, 1993).

Statutory services

Counselling and psychotherapy are increasingly being offered within NHS settings, including hospital clinics, community health centres and in GP practices. They may be offered by clinical psychologists, counselling psychologists, psychotherapists or counsellors. The psychological therapies are not always brief, sometimes entail a long waiting list and often involve specialisms within a team.

Cognitive analytic therapy was developed specifically within the NHS by Anthony Ryle in order to address the problem of waiting lists and to offer therapy more widely. Behaviour therapy has for some time been offered both at special centres like the

Institute of Psychiatry in London and in other centres. Behavioural treatment is always highly focused and naturally efficient in its use of time (Wilson, 1981). Cognitive therapy has found favour in many statutory clinical settings. All these approaches tend to be brief, CAT explicitly so. The development of counselling in primary care has not been systematic and many counsellors in such medical settings practise according to the inclinations of their training, preferred orientation and temporal habits. However, there is increasing pressure on counsellors from evaluators to examine means of making their work time limited.

Curran and Higgs (1993) suggest that 'the demand seems to be endless' for counselling in primary care settings. In their view:

> There are very rare situations where ongoing work is clearly impera-
> tive. However, offering time-limited counselling or therapy to a patient
> means that it is vitally important to get to the core of their pain and
> work at a deep level, rather than just offering a tiny and, perhaps,
> superficial bite of something which is actually meant to be much
> longer. (Curran and Higgs, 1993: 81–2)

These authors favour the application of CAT, although admitting that other approaches are also useful.

The Counselling in Primary Care Trust, obviously committed to investigating the usefulness, efficiency and evaluation of counselling in these busy settings, has endorsed the work of Cummings (1988) and Cummings and Sayama (1995), and the model of focused therapy across the life cycle. Interested readers might also consult the focused model of Pollin (1995) as well as the work of Budman and Gurman (1988).

Student counselling services

To my knowledge, most student counselling services do not operate strict time-limited policies. I know of one where a nominal five-session limit is the official policy but not the reality. Perhaps since most student counselling is characterised by an average of about four sessions for each client (Dryden and Feltham, 1992), there appears to be no need for official time limits. However, there are times when funding constraints and extra demands on these services coincide, so that waiting lists build and solutions have to be considered.

Brian Thorne (1994) recounts an experiment at the University of East Anglia. Noting that waiting lists were escalating and that five was the average number of sessions attended by students, Thorne overcame his reluctance (coming from a person-centred position), to use time-limited counselling. All students received an initial 30-minute exploratory session anyway, but some were then offered the choice of 'focused counselling', comprising three sessions of individual counselling followed by a group. Thorne found this experiment successful, covering as it did concerns ranging from delayed grief and the aftermath of rape to performance phobia and physical abuse. He notes that these clients were highly motivated, well prepared, trustful, reasonably self-accepting and articulate. What they needed was appropriate companionship on this brief therapeutic journey. In the event, the group was not run and most of the eight clients finished within the three-session contract. This is an example of a well-organised and sensitively managed experiment that had some impact on a waiting list. Thorne observes, however, that he would not condone the imposition of universal or mandatory time-limited counselling.

Traditionally, much of the ethos of student counselling in Britain stems from training in the person-centred and psychodynamic schools in the 1970s. For this reason among others, perhaps, there has been some resistance to strictly time-limited work and to those therapeutic models most likely to be concerned with the efficient use of time. Perhaps there is also a wise reluctance to extend a negatively clinical experience to people of typically student age and preferences. However, Gray (1994) and Dartington (1995) note that brief interventions with young people are often very appropriate. Coren (1996) argues that the brief counselling characteristic of student services probably meets very well the age-appropriate tasks often involved. Indeed, Coren comes out quite strongly in favour of brief therapy for a majority of students:

The high level of demand, together with the fact that counselling in educational settings is generally open access and needs to take into account the educational calendar, ensures that brief therapy is the treatment of necessity. Additionally, the majority of students only want (as opposed to what their therapists think they need) brief counselling. (Coren, 1996: 26)

Private practice

Short-term therapy may be seen as anathema to the private or independent practitioner. If you rely for your income on a steady flow of clients who attend regularly, you will not opt for short-term, time-limited work. If you did, you would find yourself having to constantly find new clients and there would be inevitable gaps in your schedule. Private practice has grown from a pattern set by Freud and others, and is intimately related to the personal finances of the therapist. Kottler captures the dilemma of the private practitioner with remarkable candour:

> When working for a public agency, the longest I ever saw a client was for fifteen to twenty sessions. At the time I thought I was doing marvelous work. It can hardly have been a coincidence that when I moved into private practice, where my livelihood depended on my ability to keep my schedule full, the average number of sessions I saw a client jumped to forty. I had, naturally, convinced myself that this longer-term approach was much better for the client; it is more intense, more elegant, more satisfying, more effective, and, yes, more costly. (1993: 190)

Kottler goes on to say that it is a lie when therapists promise to rid clients of their difficulties in the shortest possible time. Independent practitioners who rely solely or mainly on income from clients literally cannot afford a rapid throughput (Molnos, 1995: 17).

There are instances where private practitioners do engage in short-term work. These include:

1 Those who have other full-time or part-time employment (for example, lecturers, trainers, social workers) who do not need to rely on an income from private clients and who may even prefer not to be committed to long-term work.
2 Those who are retired or can depend on the income of a partner and who, therefore, may work with any client on any kind of short-term or long-term contract.
3 Those who prefer a mixture of long-term and short-term therapeutic contracts for their own reasons (for example, clinical interest or training requirements).
4 Those who take occasional time-limited referrals from EAPs or health organisations making third party payments (this is more prevalent in the USA than in Britain).

5 Those who wish to do so for specific clinical reasons (for example, they are cognitive analytic therapists) or due to political sympathies (for example, they may decide to offer short-term counselling to those people who might otherwise receive no help).

Anyone considering entering private practice should seriously reflect on the problems to be encountered in offering short-term work or in practising a clinical orientation likely to achieve rapid positive outcomes! In principle, it would seem that anyone who could gain a reputation for such outcomes might have a steady stream of paying customers. In reality, however, there are probably very few therapists gifted enough to achieve consistently brilliant outcomes. Even if you were one of these few, the costs in terms of stress may be very high.

It is worth entertaining the idea that if you do provide what you consider to be highly effective time-limited therapy, you might be morally entitled to charge higher fees accordingly. This is something advocated by McCormick (1990b), a cognitive analytic therapist who argues that the intensive nature of CAT, including between-session preparations, warrants higher charges. There is no reason why, if you intend to offer such services, you should not charge higher fees, perhaps explaining the reasons to clients verbally or in writing. Potentially, the offer of time-limited therapy with predictable charges could have a special appeal to certain clients.

Another, largely unexplored potential is for strictly time-limited, short-term therapy, including single-session therapy, as a specialism. There are clients whose work schedules do not allow for regular ongoing counselling sessions. There are clients who would prefer to pay a special, perhaps slightly longer than usual visit to a practitioner known for his or her effectiveness within a short time period. Even where this might entail considerable travel, certain clients may well be attracted by this kind of arrangement.

General considerations

Agencies considering adopting a time-limited counselling policy should always consult fully with their counsellors. Preferably, specialist training should be offered, either in-house or by funding counsellors to attend external courses. Careful thought should be given to appropriate supervision. A system of evaluation of policies, therapeutic techniques and processes, outcomes, client feedback, counsellor feedback and cost-effectiveness should ideally be implemented (Goss, 1995). Given the early stage of development of time-limited counselling in the UK, it is advisable for agency managers to convene discussion groups to examine pertinent issues, to share problems and to brainstorm solutions. It would also make sense to make connections between therapeutic time and management time, by considering time management itself as a common consideration for all concerned (Gitlin, 1990).

9

Training, Supervision, Evaluation and Research Issues

Short-term, time-limited counselling is rapidly becoming both necessary and fashionable. Probably most practitioners involved in it have learned how to do it by trial and error, since little or no specific training has been available in Britain until recently. Supervision specifically oriented to the needs of short-term counsellors is poorly developed, as I argue below. Luckily there is a reasonable amount of research to guide us in our thinking. It is to be expected that training and supervision in this area will develop rapidly, as it must if skills are to be honed. I have heard it suggested that counsellors and therapists who practise short-term, time-limited work without evidence of specific training or an affiliation with methods known to be effective in limited time spans, could be considered to be working beyond their competency and, therefore, unethically. Doubtless these problems will be clarified as time-limited work receives the attention it requires.

Training in time-limited counselling

There are still relatively few courses focusing specifically on brief and time-limited counselling and psychotherapy. Established training centres and interested associations are given in Appendix 4.

What should such courses ideally comprise? Obviously approaches with their own distinctive models of clinical procedure and explanatory theory will already be well formulated. Readers looking for training courses and trainers considering putting together courses might consider the following issues.

1 At what level should such training be devised and offered? Is it better that trainees should first have completed a lengthy training in counselling or psychotherapy? There are divided opinions on this, some arguing that time-limited work is more difficult than open-ended therapy, some arguing that it is better to approach brief counselling and therapy afresh. Cummings (1988) argues that experienced long-term practitioners need extra training because time-limited work requires well-honed decision-making skills; it does not provide the opportunity to return, in leisurely fashion, time and time again to the same issues for resolution. Rosen (1990) is essentially in agreement with this position. Rawson (1992), however, argues that effective focal therapy requires a previous mastery of a variety of therapeutic approaches; she offsets against this the argument that newcomers to short-term counselling may be freer of resistance to it.

2 Should the brief nature of time-limited counselling be reflected in a brief training? Clearly this relates to point 1 above insofar as the answer depends on the previous training of candidates. In principle, if funders were minded to train large numbers of time-limited counsellors economically, I would see no objection to brief training, provided that such a training contained significant input on assessment and referral elements. Otherwise, if brief counselling or psychotherapy were to be seen as the norm rather than the exception, then I would say that training would need to be of similar length as current courses. However, as Molnos (1995: 14) reminds us, 'training programmes grow longer year by year as training institutions for counsellors and psychotherapists increase their requirements in order to approximate their ideal of the prestigious training for long-term psychoanalysis.'

3 What are the essential ingredients of a training in time-limited counselling? Like any other course, an historical overview is useful (although not essential), setting the approach in context. Time should be devoted to airing all issues relating to time-limited counselling, including contentious issues. Economic arguments for the place of such an approach are important and possibly a module on cost-effectiveness would be a helpful inclusion.

Philosophical and ethical questions should be addressed. Greater attention to fundamental questions of the nature of therapy than is customary would be helpful, and it seems inevitable that trainers and trainees ask which among the current plethora of models offers satisfactory explanations of human distress; unavoidably, I believe, any training in time-limited counselling must take a somewhat flexible approach, incorporating some theoretical integration and some technical eclecticism (Budman and Gurman, 1988; Garfield, 1995; Cummings and Sayama, 1995).

Assessment, referral, psychiatric and medical issues are crucial. Research, including that on clients' experiences and views, is a useful part of an ideal training. However, of central importance in any course of this kind must be the exploration of key technical ingredients and facilitative aspects of the therapeutic relationship. Strupp (1990) suggests that training in interpersonal awareness is a crucial ingredient in time-limited therapy, since many clients are lost by the third session if a satisfactory alliance has not been established. Cade and O'Hanlon (1993: 16) place a major emphasis on learning by doing (solution-focused brief therapy), 'on practice rather than on theory'. Finally, in my view, a critical module that should be incorporated is one in which questions are posed about the myths and limits of, and contraindications for, time-limited counselling.

4 How can time-limited counselling be practised? Apart from the kind of role play and personal development groups already familiar on many training courses (which could be adapted to focus on brief interventions), clinical practice may be gained in many of the settings currently used as counsellor placements (for example, student counselling services, voluntary agencies). In addition, some GP practices already permit coun- sellor trainees to take up placement opportunities. Ideally, where trainees are mature people with at least some previous training, access should be given to placements within primary care settings, in employee counselling services and elsewhere.

5 Should personal experience of time-limited counselling in the client role be a prerequisite for training? Since one of the arguments for insisting upon or strongly encouraging engagement in personal therapy for trainees is that it introduces them to what it actually feels like to be a client, it follows logically that trainees on a time-limited counselling course would benefit from com- parable experiences. Indeed, I believe this is the case. While some experience could be gained within dyadic role plays within training, using counsellors external to the course for focused time-limited work on oneself would almost certainly enhance understanding and commitment.

Some exercises and questions to develop awareness of attitudes towards the meaning and use of time are given below. The purpose is to challenge attitudes and to stimulate discussion.

1   Have students construct a life-chart – a simple line, beginning at birth and marked with significant life events. Ask them to project into the future what they expect or hope to achieve by what ages, and when they expect to die. Ask them also to construct an alternative line of development that might be facilitated by serendipitous events or therapeutic change. Encourage dyadic and whole-group sharing of experiences, feelings and beliefs.

2   At what times, in what circumstances in your own and students' lives has time seemed to pass very slowly and very rapidly? Compare experiences.

3   Have each student consider some undesirable or unattractive personal habit he or she is aware of (for example, overeating, overspending, excessive drinking, procrastination, social anxiety, poor hygiene, lack of assertiveness, etc.). How long has it operated? How often have attempts been made to lessen or eradicate it? How long would it take to change it in therapy? How long does the person propose to tolerate it?

4   Consider the expression 'If I'd known then what I know now, I would have acted very differently'. Imagining yourself in the future (say, 10 years from now), wiser, more experienced, free of most current fears, what would that future self say to the current troubled self to help them change?

5   Have students sit still and upright with their eyes closed and their breathing calm. Run through a muscular relaxation exercise from head to toes. Repeat several times, 'Time has ceased to matter' and 'You are sitting between the past which has gone and the future which never arrives'. Ask, 'Does your body inhabit a past or future?'. On opening their eyes, have the students move around the room without speech. Discuss and compare the concepts of timelessness and the relentless passing of time.

6 Compare the following statements: (a) I will never be able to fly like a bird; (b) I will never be a millionaire; (c) I will never live to be 100; (d) I will probably never be able to overcome my most stubborn personal problem/habit/fear.

7 Role-play a counselling situation in which, unknown to each other (use role play cards), the counsellor has recently learned that she has a terminal illness and the client has only one session in which to try to extract a letter confirming high levels of stress necessitating time off work. Try variants on this mismatch scenario.

8 Role-play a counselling situation in which the counsellor is under pressure from his or her manager to bring things to an end and the client stalls, brings up worrying new material, and so on.

9 Separate the group into two. Have each compete against the other in completing the following task. A proposal for a publisher has to be written for a book on time-limited counselling, including arguments supporting the rationale of the book, any similar books already published, likely readership and market, indicative chapters, length of the book and proposed deadline for its delivery. Thirty minutes is the maximum time allowed for this task but the group finishing first get credit for that. The winner is finally judged on quality too.

10 Role-play the following situation. A panel of administrators have asked for a presentation on why they should fund a new generic counselling service and how costs can be controlled by very short-term counselling in all cases. Two students (who have been given time to marshal their arguments and who believe that every client should get exactly how long they need) make this presentation and meet the counter-arguments of the panel (who have also been given time to develop their objections).

11 A volunteer is needed to present an actual personal problem to the rest of the group. Everyone is free to respond. This is treated as an actual session. The following week a second session is provided. A gap in time is then built in; after some weeks a follow-up session is conducted. The goal is concrete, measurable progress. Alternatively, this exercise may be conducted in small groups.

12 Students, arranged in small groups, are asked to brainstorm ways in which therapy can be made as protracted as possible

with a particular client. Collate all suggestions and discuss. This is, of course, a paradoxical exercise!

13   Have students use the empty chair technique to explore opposing temporal attitudes. For example, one part of you may think, 'Yes, I can do it, I can and I will change today, no time is required.', while another thinks, 'This is very hard for me, very painful, and I need time, as much time as it takes, to get through it.' Encourage dialogue between these parts, or variants on them, so that the emotive issues involved in time-limited counselling emerge and can be discussed afterwards.

Time and *counselling skills* is also an area that warrants at least a brief mention. By this I refer to the fact that people learning counselling skills on short courses often need to apply those skills in precisely the kinds of setting where time is scarce, or is not allocated for lengthy counselling encounters. A group of physio-therapy students who I once taught some counselling skills to, for example, told me that they would never have time to engage in counselling-type interactions because their jobs were too busy. It became apparent after some discussion, however, that even where there are only two spare minutes with a client the worker has a *choice* about how she or he responds – with silence, formal politeness, social chit-chat; or empathy, challenge or problem-solving strategies. The argument that 'there's no time' is never literally true. Quite often, there is very little time. But even in moments we can waste opportunities. Awareness of what time-limited counselling skills have to offer could be an important ingredient in the training of all helping professionals.

Supervision

The practice of short-term, time-limited counselling presents intriguing challenges to supervisors for two main reasons. First, many supervisors – simply by virtue of the fact that they are senior practitioners – have specialised in their own training in the longer-term, relationship-based models like psychodynamic and person-centred counselling or therapy. I have certainly come across supervisors who regard the newer short-term approaches with some disdain. Secondly, it is in the very nature of short-term work that it may, in effect, be over or all but completed by the time the counsellor attends his or her next supervision session.

Those receiving supervision on a fortnightly, three-weekly or monthly basis may have some clients for three or four sessions and hardly have the chance to take these cases to supervision at all (except for a post-mortem). Alternatively, they may discuss them just once or twice in supervision but barely have time to use that supervisory input meaningfully. Exactly how single-session therapy can be meaningfully supervised also presents intriguing challenges.

Supervision of time-limited counselling, therefore, throws up some interesting challenges. This is confirmed by Graham Curtis Jenkins, Director of the Counselling in Primary Care Trust, who reports that in Britain and in the USA it is often difficult for brief therapists to find suitable supervisors; that much of their supervision is inappropriate; and that they sometimes have to 'conceal from their supervisors how they are working for fear of evoking rebuke and scorn!' (Curtis Jenkins, personal communication, 1996).

The design of supervision courses must take this problem into account. Trainee supervisors must be faced with any reservations they may have about short-term work and they should be provided with case examples and/or role play in dealing with short-term clients. (Significantly, most of the literature on supervision seems to be built on the assumption of fairly long-term counselling, with time for leisurely reflection on the therapeutic process.) If supervisors themselves have done little or no short-term, time-limited work, this might become a requirement of such courses: if you have not experienced the challenges of this work yourself, how will you effectively supervise those who encounter it daily, or at least frequently? A counsellor grappling with the peculiar features of time-limited counselling would no doubt appreciate help from a supervisor who can understand the challenges and offer constructive suggestions.

What is the solution to the conundrum of the supervision of the rapid turnover of short-term clients? With luck, you may get to discuss each of your short-term clients (supposing you see them for, say, six or eight sessions) once or twice in supervision, unless you happen to have frequent (weekly) supervision. Ironically, the challenge of effective short-term counselling may, in fact, imply that *extra* supervision is required. In other words, if you are to offer maximum therapeutic potency in a short time, perhaps you need maximum support and stimulation yourself. This kind of intensive supervisory input may be achievable in certain agencies but I doubt whether it is currently widely available. Ideally, practitioners would receive opportunities for virtually on-the-spot supervision (as is provided in certain family therapy formats). Supervision utilising tape-recordings, video-recordings or, at the very least, process notes made soon after sessions, should be provided within a meaningful time after the counselling session, allowing for consideration of how to approach the next session. If this is not practicable in certain settings, it should at least be provided during the training period for time-limited work. Weekly group supervision is considered extremely important in cognitive analytic therapy, particularly in the formative period and particularly in relation to the first four sessions of client contact (Ryle, 1990).

I am aware of two particular areas in which time sensitivity features in supervision. First, in facilitated group supervision the task of dividing available time (say, two hours between four supervisees) often falls to the supervisor. There is then a certain onus to utilise each supervisee's half hour optimally, vigilantly monitoring any tendencies for other supervisees to take over or for the focus to be lost to peripheral issues. Secondly, some transactional analysis supervisors (in groups or in individual supervision) will contract with supervisees exactly how super-vision time is to be used. For example, 'You have 20 minutes, Sian. How would you like to use it?' may form the basis of a mini-contract for a particular supervision session. In this case the supervisee, Sian, may be asked to specify precisely which issue she wishes to work on. Many supervisors, in addition, agree with supervisees at the beginning of each session how much time they wish to spend discussing particular clients or themes. All these temporal aspects of supervision may be used to model ways in which time can be managed in time-limited counselling.

Of the few available references to supervision of time-limited work, Cade and O'Hanlon (1993) suggest that (solution-focused) brief therapy should be subject to live supervision from the beginning of training. In a supervision transcript provided by Holloway (1995: 18), the supervisor suggests that the supervisee is thinking that the client might need to hear, 'Hey, you are using up airtime with storytelling that doesn't seem to be the point of what our goals are here.' One of the ways in which supervisors can certainly help is at the assessment stage, assisting the counsellor in decisions about the suitability of time-limited work with particular clients. Kramer (1989: 84) cites an example of his supervisor recommending a stringently 12-session therapy for a client who, having had previous therapies, appeared likely to act out in a placatory and seductive fashion, for example.

Evaluation

Reflecting on your own work and getting feedback from clients and supervisors are perhaps the main sources of evaluation. All of us to some extent reflect fleetingly on what we are doing within the session itself, as well as immediately after the session and, perhaps, from time to time between sessions. If you make regular in-depth notes you will be particularly inclined to identify any areas of concern, interest or satisfaction. Asking your client periodically or regularly for feedback is another means of evaluating your work (Dryden and Feltham, 1994). If you or your agency wish to seek formal or rigorous evaluation, questionnaires or interviews may be used but always present ethical dilemmas.

The kinds of question you may find it helpful to put to yourself immediately after a session or when reviewing an audiotape of one of your sessions include:

1 Have I made it clear to the client from the outset to what extent we are working within a non-negotiable (or, if appropriate, negotiable) limited time frame?
2 Have I generally established a sense of urgency, expectation and hope?
3 In this session, did I sensitively apply an appropriate degree of temporal pressure?
4 Can I distinguish between my own wasteful passivity in this session and necessary or fruitful pauses, silences, etc.?
5 Exactly what did I do in this session which helped to move matters forward?
6 What was the focal or recurring content of this session?
7 What opportunities did I miss in the session?
8 Did I at any point inappropriately hurry or pressurise the client?
9 In what way was this session related productively to the client's presenting and persisting goals?

10　What evidence is there that the client is moving towards his or her goals?

11　What remains to be done in future sessions?

12　Do I have any specific strategies or opening statements for the next session?

13　Are there any signs that short-term counselling is unhelpful for this client or that alternative approaches may be indicated?

The kinds of question you may wish to put to clients either verbally or in questionnaire format include:

1　Was it made clear to you at the outset that you were being offered time-limited counselling?

2　Was this genuinely acceptable to you or did you feel that you had no choice?

3　In what ways did the counsellor help to orientate you to counselling and how to use it actively?

4　Were you able to identify reasonably clear goals or aims in your counselling?

5　Have you been satisfied with your counsellor's efforts to help you achieve your goals and aims?

6　To what extent are you either pleased with the progress you have made, or dissatisfied?

7　Have you at any time found the time limits problematic or distressing?

8　What do you think the key ingredients in the helpfulness of your counselling have been?

9　Would you recommend this counsellor to your friends?

10　What might improve the effectiveness of the counsellor and/ or the kind of counselling you have received?

Some research issues

Barkham (1990) has succinctly presented a number of points on the length of therapy. He mentions that the longest recorded length of any therapy is 1,114 sessions (Weiss and Sampson, 1986). He discusses the dose-effect curve, which shows that 14 per cent of clients are likely to improve even before attending their first session; 24 per cent are likely to have improved by the end of the first session; 30 per cent by the second session; 41 per cent by the fourth; 53 per cent by the eighth; 62 per cent by the thirteenth; 74 per cent by the twenty-sixth; 83 per cent by session 52; and 90 per cent at 104 sessions (*see* Howard et al., 1986). What can be inferred from these figures is that two-thirds of clients are helped significantly within 13 sessions or so. Certainly a great many people can be helped within a relatively short time, whereas there are diminishing returns after a certain period of therapy.

Smith et al.'s (1980) meta-analysis of outcome studies concluded, among other things, that therapeutic success did not depend significantly on the length of therapy. Short-term therapy could be as effective as long-term therapy. This apparent equivalence has been noted by Koss and Butcher (1986), who also provide supporting evidence for many other brief therapy claims. We also know that the mean length of therapy as actually experienced by clients has repeatedly been calculated as being around six sessions (Budman and Gurman, 1988; Garfield, 1995). This figure does not reflect every client population; Carlson (1995: 13) estimates that people who attend his Californian stress management centre have on average had at least 100 hours of previous (unsuccessful) therapy. I have referred earlier to the finding that many counsellors reckon that clients need at least three times the amount of therapy that clients themselves think they need (Pekarik and Finney-Owen, 1987).

There is evidence that significant therapeutic gains, using both cognitive–behavioural and exploratory (relationship-oriented) approaches can be made in three sessions (Barkham, 1990). In one research sample it was found that 78 per cent of clients who received single-session therapy were satisfied with what they had received (Talmon, 1990). Overall, a large amount of data suggest that short-term therapy is wanted or preferred, is appreciated and perceived as successful. This does not lead to the conclusion that we should all be immediately converted to the practice of the shortest possible therapy, but we ignore such findings at our peril.

What are the kinds of issues we might be researching in this field? What would we like to know more about? Based on my own experience and a small survey of practising counsellors, some of the most pertinent issues may be:

1   What kind of training should be developed for time-limited counsellors, based on the question: what problems and issues do counsellors typically encounter in time-limited work?

2   What evidence is there to support the view that certain kinds of personalities and client problems, or clusters of problems, are more and less suitable for time-limited therapy?

3   How can we find out more about client readiness and motivation, and about optimal timing for therapeutic interventions?

4   Is there evidence suggesting that there are identifiable interventions which achieve greater or more rapid and enduring change than others or than the contributions of non-specific relationship factors?

5   Are there any indications as to whether hour-long weekly sessions, or more or less frequent sessions, or spaced or massed sessions may be more effective?

6   Are there indications of any 'magic numbers' in planned time-limited counselling (in other words, is there an optimal number of sessions suited to most presenting issues)?

7   What evidence exists to suggest that clients who have received short-term therapy relapse later or even deteriorate?

8   To what extent can the costs of time-limited counselling be predicted and used as an argument in changing provision of counselling services generally?

9   How can we investigate qualitatively the processes involved in time-limited counselling?

10 How can we investigate philosophically and critically the many temporal questions thrown up by the challenge of time-limited counselling?

Appendix 1

Psychotherapists in Dialogue with Krishnamurti

Following the conference of scientists with Krishnamurti at Brockwood Park last October, one of the participants, Dr. David Shainberg, offered to arrange a similar meeting with a group of American psychotherapists. This took place in the form of a two-day dialogue which was held in New York City in late April. The following report on this meeting, written especially for the Bulletin by Dr. Shainberg, contains material of exceptional interest and merits close attention. Dr. Shainberg, practising psychiatrist, is Assistant Dean of the Specialty Program in Psychoanalytic Medicine, Postgraduate Center for Mental Health, New York City.

On April 29, 30, 1975, Krishnamurti met in New York City with twenty-five psychotherapists. The group represented a variety of theoretical orientations, including those of Freud, Horney, Sullivan, and Rogers. There were four social workers, four psychologists, and seventeen psychiatrists. There were several directors of psychoanalytic training institutes, a director of a hospital department of psychiatry, many professors, and several people who have contributed extensively to psychoanalytic knowledge.

This group assembled to explore the relationships and implications of Krishnamurti's teaching for their daily work. Each person well knew the difficulty involved in helping another human being. From the moment the discussion began the atmosphere of the dialogue was intense, deeply serious and respectful.

Appropriately, the first issue raised was: What is the root of fear? A useful distinction immediately emerged: there is a biological concern in which we know about fires, snakes, etc. Some called this the domain of 'practical fear'. Krishnamurti pointed out that this is not psychological fear, but is an 'intelligence of self preservation.' Psychological fear is different. Krishnamurti stressed that psychological fear is caused by thinking. Becoming, he said, with its fear of *not* becoming, is the root of all fear. 'If there were no thinking, there would be no fear.' One psychiatrist responded, 'If there were no thinking, you would not be human.' But Krishnamurti urged the discussion toward considering the possibility of no thinking as being truly human. There was initial difficulty in understanding this, but the group began to get at the heart of the dilemma as Krishnamurti emphasized the need to go to the root of fear, not to its branches. Fear and its branches always arise when, instead of immediate action, there is thinking as becoming.

Psychotherapists customarily focus on the thoughts of their patients or, if not on the thoughts, on becoming and being. The therapist tries to help the patient become less fearful, more mature, more adept in society. So it was something of a shock for many of the participants in this dialogue to consider that thought and becoming were the root of mental disease. But to many it was more than shocking, often very deeply confusing, when Krishnamurti pointed out that being itself was the deepest root of fear. Few understood, but all were wondering. Krishnamurti asked how is it possible to prevent disease altogether?

From there the group moved to a central difference: Psychotherapists, and of course the whole world, are accustomed to think in terms of process. This implies that it takes time to change, time for any transformation to occur. One man, for example, said that Krishnamurti's point about the transforming of consciousness seemed to imply a process. Patients, it was argued, get better 'over time' as a result of participation in a dialogue we call therapy. It can be observed that these patients have less fear as the result of a change in their knowledge about themselves and about the world. How, the therapists wondered, is it possible to throw out the idea of process when they see this betterment over time happen so often? Krishnamurti wondered if such people did not actually pick up another dependency to alleviate their fears. He asked: Is it possible to be totally free of fear and not simply to have less fear (as was suggested is the usual result of psychotherapy)?

This kind of question came up in another form in a discussion about development, a concept which attracts the interest of most therapists. Central to psychoanalytic theories is the idea that the child develops in time and that diseases of the mind emerge in faulty accomplishment of various developmental tasks over the course of a process. Similarly, the therapist observes a process in the patient who gradually resolves his various fears. As the therapy progresses there are changes; different fears emerge into the foreground. The patient is gradually able to extend his life and live more 'productively' and more 'freely'. Krishnamurti agreed that the organism as such has undergone development. But the organism is different from the 'me'. This me is a product of thought as an avoidance of immediate action. The me or self, which therapists focus on, is a feature of the process of becoming and is the disease itself with its incessant need to be.

Krishnamurti stressed that we do not act in the moment. We therefore have concepts which are conclusions about the moment; these concepts are the basis on which we act. But if action occurs instantaneously the issue is finished. This under-standing questions the way therapists live and work with patients. It asks them if they are communicating through thought as knowledge, memory, concepts, and theories. Was therapy possible under such auspices? Or is it necessary to have an immediate communication outside the field of thought? In fact, Krishnamurti led the participants to consider if it is possible to use knowledge at all to communicate in the field of the self, sorrow, and conflict.

This also raised questions about the kind of change seen in patients whom the therapist considers improved. Though they may get 'better' at adapting to this corrupt world, does that mean they are able to love or are free of fear? This also raised questions about the traditional concept of maturity. By some, growth and maturity is considered to be the accumulation of learning through time. Krishnamurti asked if there is an action which is not of the me or of time. Does that have anything to do with knowledge and learning? And is love in any way related to knowledge?

The issue of process came up in another way when one therapist noted: 'We see a lot of patients who feel like they are nothing. That is, they are, as you suggest, feeling empty of the me and of the content of consciousness.' Krishnamurti observed that the problem with such people is that they are really feeling they want to be something. Another doctor felt this was more of a problem than Krishnamurti had implied. He insisted that this state of feeling nothing was *because* these patients were afraid. It was not the result of overcoming fear. It was a state *before* feeling, experiencing, or contact with life. This doctor and others felt it was necessary for the patient to go through a process of experiencing a me, a self, before he could let go of the me.

Krishnamurti kept pointing out that no process is necessary in order to be aware of the nature of thought and becoming, or of the formation of ideals, and that the interval between what is and the inventions of thought is to be instantaneously finished with. He challenged another basic psychoanalytic assumption by asserting that it is unnecessary through time to disclose the deep layers of the unconscious. The therapists felt that a process of such revealing was necessary, but Krishnamurti said complete attention to the moment of action is all-inclusive action and is sufficient. It was clear that therapists felt that patients were not capable of attending to the moment, and that they needed preparation in order to gradually realize the limits of thought, including help in going through a process of accentuating the self.

So throughout the dialogue the recurrent theme was how to find an action which is beyond time and thought. It was disturbing for many to hear that it was impossible to act consciously without fragmenting, and that truth had nothing whatever to do with reality which is the product of thought. Implicit in the discussion and often emerging in explicit bursts was the question: How can psychotherapists help their patients if they are not whole themselves? Of course everyone in the room was aware of his own fragmentation and this confronted everyone with questions of what kind of helping they were doing.

To explore this, Krishnamurti emphasized that there is no psychological security. The action of thinking and becoming is the action of insecurity. The only security is the full realization there is no psychological security. In the realization of this, thought and becoming come to an end. This discussion challenged the analysis process in which most participants engaged daily. Krishnamurti observed that analysis as thought was a paralysis of action. It goes from one part to the next part, endlessly incomplete. Acting from conclusion to conclusion produces endless fragmentation and is itself a process of fragmentation; it is all an action of thought. It can never move to freedom.

Several therapists present appreciated that Krishnamurti had shown that the patient's tendency to talk *about* himself was being supported and aided by the use of thought in endless analysis.

Many in the group became deeply interested in whether there is a whole action which is beyond time and thought. Participants found it disturbing to consider that truth lies beyond thinking.

Krishnamurti suggested that when two people in dialogue both realized they were not whole, there was no longer an observer and an observed, no authority, no patient and doctor, with all the division that implied; then the whole came into being in the act of participation. So love, which is beyond thought and analysing, is the action of perception; an action which is not time-binding.

Most of the psychotherapists who attended the two-day conference were deeply moved by the discussion. In general they had great difficulty understanding that no process was necessary. This challenged the psychoanalytic assumptions of growth and development. To be nothing and to live directly in the moment intrigued and interested many who appreciated that the endless analysis through thought was not helping their patients. Many reported they were stirred, and moved to question; some said they felt more tranquil after the work with Krishnamurti. One man said 'It was like a breath of fresh air.' But it is clear that further dialogue is necessary to comprehend the process of thought.

Appendix 2

The Psychotherapy File – An aid to understanding ourselves better

We have all had just one life and what has happened to us, and the sense we made of this colours the way we see ourselves and others. How we see things is for us, how things are, and how we go about our lives seems 'obvious and right'. Sometimes, however, our familiar ways of understanding and acting can be the source of our problems. In order to solve our difficulties we may need to learn to recognise how what we do makes things worse. We can then work out new ways of thinking and acting.

These pages are intended to suggest ways of thinking about what you do; Recognising your particular patterns is the first step in learning to gain more control and happiness in your life.

Keeping a diary of your moods and behaviour

Symptoms, bad moods, unwanted thoughts or behaviours that come and go can be better understood and controlled if you learn to notice when they happen and what starts them off.

If you have a particular symptom or problem of this sort, start keeping a diary. The diary should be focused on a particular mood, symptom or behaviour, and should be kept every day if possible. Try to record this sequence:

1   How you were feeling about yourself and others and the world *before* the problem came on.
2   Any external event, or any thought or image in your mind, that was going on when the trouble started, or what seemed to start if off.
3   Once the trouble started, what were the thoughts, images or feelings you experienced.

By noticing and writing down in this way what you do and think at these times, you will learn to recognise – and eventually have more control over – how you act and think at the time. It is often the case that bad feelings like resentment, depression or physical symptoms are the result of ways of thinking and acting that are unhelpful. Diary-keeping in this way gives you the chance to learn better ways of dealing with things.

It is helpful to keep a diary record for 1–2 weeks, then to discuss what you have recorded with your therapist or counsellor.

Patterns that do not work, but are hard to break

There are certain ways of thinking and acting that do not achieve what we want, but which are hard to change. Read through the lists on the following pages and mark how far you think they apply to you.

Applies strongly + +   Applies +   Does not apply 0

TRAPS

Traps are things we cannot escape from. Certain kinds of thinking and acting result in a 'vicious circle' when, however hard we try, things seem to get worse instead of better. Trying to deal with feeling bad about ourselves, we think and act in ways that tend to confirm our badness.

Examples of Traps

1 Fear of hurting others Trap

Feeling fearful of hurting others* we keep our feelings inside, or put our own needs aside. This tends to allow other people to ignore or abuse us in various ways, which then leads to our feeling, or being, childishly angry. When we see ourselves behaving like this, it confirms our belief that we shouldn't be aggressive and reinforces our avoidance of standing up for our rights.

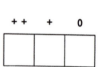

* *People often get trapped in this way because they mix up aggression and assertion. Mostly, being assertive – asking for our rights – is perfectly acceptable. People who do not respect our rights as human beings must either be stood up to or avoided.*

2 Depressed thinking Trap

Feeling depressed, we are sure we will manage a task or social situation badly. Being depressed, we are probably not as effective as we can be, and the depression leads us to exaggerate how badly we handled things. This makes us feel more depressed about ourselves.

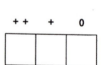

3 Trying to please Trap

Feeling uncertain about ourselves and anxious not to upset others, we try to please people by doing what they seem to want. As a result (1) we end up being taken advantage of by others which makes us angry, depressed or guilty, from which our uncertainty about ourselves is confirmed; or (2) sometimes we feel out of control because of the need to please, and start hiding away, putting things off, letting people down, which makes other people angry with us and increases our uncertainty.

4 Avoidance Trap

We feel ineffective and anxious about certain situations, such as crowded streets, open spaces, social gatherings. We try to go back into these situations, but feel even more anxiety. Avoiding them makes us feel better, so we stop trying. However, by constantly avoiding situations our lives are limited and we come to feel increasingly ineffective and anxious.

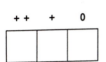

5 Social isolation Trap

Feeling under-confident about ourselves and anxious not to upset others, we worry that others will find us boring or stupid, so we don't look at people or respond to friendliness. People then see us as unfriendly, so we become more isolated from which we are convinced we are boring and stupid – and become more under-confident.

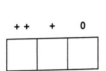

6 Low self-esteem Trap

Feeling worthless, we feel that we cannot get what we want because (a) we will be punished, (b) others will reject or abandon us, or (c) as if anything good we get is bound to go away or turn sour. Sometimes it feels as if we must punish ourselves for being weak. From this we feel that everything is hopeless, so we give up trying to do anything – which confirms and increases our sense of worthlessness.

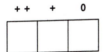

DILEMMAS (False choices and narrow options)

We often act as we do, even when we are not completely happy with it, because the only other ways we can imagine, seem as bad or even worse. Sometimes we assume connections that are not necessarily the case – as in 'if I do *x* then *y* will follow'. These *false choices* can be described as either/or or if/then *dilemmas*.

We often don't realise that we see things like this, but we act as if these were the only possible choices.

Do you act as if any of the following false choices rule your life? Recognising them is the first step to changing them.

Choices about myself
I act AS IF:

1   Either I keep feelings bottled up or I risk being rejected, hurting others, or making a mess.

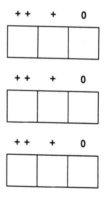

2   Either I feel I spoil myself and am greedy or I deny myself things and punish myself and feel miserable.

3   If I try to be perfect, I feel depressed and angry: If I don't try to be perfect, I feel guilty, angry and dissatisfied.

4   If I must then I won't; it is as if when faced with a task I must either gloomily submit or passively resist (other people's wishes, or even my own feel too demanding, so I put things off, avoid them).

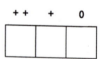

5   If I must not then I will; it is as if the only proof of my existence is my resistance (other people's rules, or even my own feel too restricting, so I break rules and do things which are harmful to me).

6   If other people aren't expecting me to do things, look after them etc., then I feel anxious, lonely and out of control.

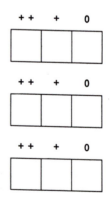

7   If I get what I want I feel childish and guilty; If I don't get what I want, I feel frustrated, angry and depressed.

8   Either I keep things (feelings, plans) in perfect order, or I fear a terrible mess.

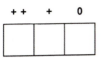

Choices about how we relate to others
I behave with others AS IF:

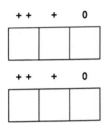

1   Either I'm involved with someone and likely to get hurt, or I don't get involved and stay in charge, but remain lonely.

2   Either I stick up for myself and nobody likes me, or I give in and get put on by others and feel cross and hurt.

3   I'm either a brute or a martyr (secretly blaming the other).

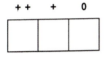

4   (a) With others either I'm safely wrapped up in bliss or in combat.
(b) If in combat, then I'm either a bully or a victim.

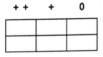

5   Either I look down on other people, or I feel they look down on me.

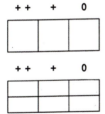

6   (a) Either I'm sustained by the admiration of others whom I admire, or I feel exposed.
(b) If exposed, then I feel either contemptuous of others or I feel contemptible.

7   Either I'm involved with others and feel engulfed, taken over or smothered, or I stay safe and uninvolved but feel lonely and isolated.

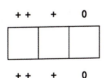

8   When I'm involved with someone whom I care about then either I have to give in or they have to give in.

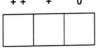

9 When I'm involved with someone whom I depend on, then either I have to give in or they have to give in.

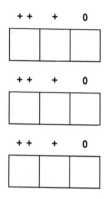

10 As a woman, either I have to do what others want or I stand up for my rights and get rejected.

11 As a man, either I can't have any feelings or I am an emotional mess.

SNAGS

Snags are what is happening when we say 'I want to have a better life, or I want to change my behaviour but . . .'. Sometimes this comes from how we or our families thought about us when we were young; such as 'She was always the good child', or 'In our family we never . . .'. Sometimes the snags come from the important people in our lives not wanting us to change, or not able to cope with what our changing means to them. Often the resistance is more indirect, as when a parent, husband or wife becomes ill or depressed when we begin to get better.

In other cases, we seem to 'arrange' to avoid pleasure or success, or if they come, we have to pay in some way, by depression, or by spoiling things. Often this is because, as children, we came to feel guilty if things went well for us, or felt that we were envied for good luck or success. Sometimes we have come to feel responsible, unreasonably, for things that went wrong in the family, although we may not be aware that this is so. It is helpful to learn to recognise how this sort of pattern is stopping you getting on with your life, for only then can you learn to accept your right to a better life and begin to claim it.

You may get quite depressed when you begin to realise how often you stop your life being happier and more fulfilled. It is important to remember that it's not being stupid or bad, but rather that:

1 We do these things because this is the way we learned to manage best when we were younger.

2 We don't have to keep on doing them now we are learning to recognise them.

3 By changing our behaviour, we can learn not only to control our own behaviour, but also how to change the way other people behave towards us.

4 Although it may seem that others resist the changes we want for ourselves (for example, our parents, or our partners), we often under-estimate them. If we are firm about our right to change, those who care for us will usually accept the change.

Do you recognise that you feel limited in your life:

1 For fear of the response of others? (For example, success *as if* it deprives others, *as if* others may envy me, or *as if* there are not enough good things to go around.)

2 By something inside yourself? (For example, I must sabotage good things *as if* I don't deserve them.)

DIFFICULT AND UNSTABLE STATES OF MIND

Some people find it difficult to keep control over their behaviour and experience because things feel very difficult and different at times. Indicate which, if any, of the following apply to you:

1 How I feel about myself and others can be unstable; I can switch from one state of mind to a completely different one.

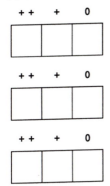

2 Some states may be accompanied by intense, extreme and uncontrollable emotions.

3 Other states may be accompanied by emotional blankness, feeling unreal, or feeling muddled.

4 Some states are accompanied by feeling intensely guilty or angry with myself, wanting to hurt myself.

+ +	+	0

5 Other states are accompanied by feeling that others can't be trusted, are going to let me down, or hurt me.

+ +	+	0

6 Yet other states are accompanied by being unreasonably angry or hurtful to others.

+ +	+	0

7 Sometimes the only way to cope with some confusing feelings is to blank them off and feel emotionally distant from others.

+ +	+	0

Appendix 3

Sample Agency Policy Explanation

What is counselling?

Counselling is one way of trying to help people discuss and think through personal concerns with the aim of finding relief, greater understanding and some resolution of difficulties. It is a confidential arrangement characterised by conversation, but is usually more than 'just a chat' because you are invited to be as honest and open as possible. Counsellors are trained to listen attentively, to help you identify the subtleties of your concerns, to be non-judgemental and to help you regain your own self-determination. There are different schools of thought underpinning counselling practice, and sometimes people with different professional titles are in fact offering the same kind of help.

What is time-limited counselling?

Evidence shows that while some people only want to see a counsellor once, others want to attend weekly sessions for months or even years. Some research suggests that average attendance is around six or eight sessions. Often the greatest gains are made in counselling within the first few sessions. Sometimes people put off dealing with difficult issues in their lives and spend a long time in counselling that may not always be useful. Obviously the more people there are who are engaged in long-term counselling, the longer waiting lists grow. For all these, and other reasons this agency operates a policy of limiting or structuring time available for counselling.

What is available to you?

Everyone who comes to us for counselling has initial access to eight free sessions of counselling, usually for one hour on a weekly basis. If you decide not to use all sessions available to you, please let us know that you are not returning and always feel free to contact us again at a later stage. If you use all eight sessions and are still in need of further counselling you may negotiate another six sessions. Your counsellor will review with you any further needs you may have after that time. In some cases it may be more helpful for you to be directed to alternative, specialist sources of counselling or psychotherapy. In some instances, you may decide with your counsellor that a double (two hour) session is more useful to you, or that fortnightly or occasional sessions best meet your needs. While it is important for us to be realistic and disciplined about the resources available to us – including time – we are always concerned with individual needs.

How can you make the best use of your counselling?

You may appreciate that we wish to make the best use we can of the therapeutic time available. Experience suggests that the following key features assist people in getting the most out of time-limited counselling:

- Contact us when the time is right for you, when you sense that your need is greatest and your motivation highest.
- Agree on one or two reasonably well-focused personal concerns or goals with your counsellor.
- Let us or your counsellor know if at any stage you feel the counselling is not right for you.
- Co-operate with any reasonable suggestions the counsellor makes about trying out new behaviour or doing 'homework'.
- Accept that everyone finds change difficult and that counselling often feels like a mixture of risk, resistance and hard work.

- Use the opportunity of counselling by expressing your inner-most thoughts and feelings freely.
- Build bridges between your counselling and everyday life by reading relevant books, seeking out social support and challenge.

Appendix 4

Organisations offering training in or information on short-term counselling or psychotherapy

Association of Cognitive Analytic
  Therapists
CAT Training Secretary
Munro Clinic
Guy's Hospital
London SE1 9RT
0171 955 2906

Association of Short-term and
  Strategic Psychotherapists/
  FASTPACE (The Focal and Short-
  Term Psychotherapy Centre)
194 Emlyn Road
London W12 9TB
0181 749 7970

The Brief Therapy Practice
4d Shirland Mews
London W9 3DY
0181 968 0070

British Association for Behavioural
  and Cognitive Psychotherapies
c/o Rod Holland
Harrow Psychological Health
  Services
Northwick Park Hospital
Watford Road
Harrow
Middlesex
HA1 3UJ
0181 869 2326

Centre for Multimodal Therapy/
  Centre for Rational Emotive
  Behaviour Therapy
156 Westcombe Hill
London SE3 7DH
0181 293 4114

Centre for Reality Therapy
The Green House
43 George Street
Leighton Buzzard
Bedfordshire
LU7 8JX
01525 851588

Counselling Development Unit
School of Education
Sheffield Hallam University
Collegiate Crescent
Sheffield S10 2BP
0114 2532245

Counselling in Primary Care Trust
Majestic House
High Street
Staines TW18 4DG
01784 441782

Psychological Therapies Research
  Centre
Attn. Dr Michael Barkham
17 Blenheim Terrace
University of Leeds
Leeds LS2 9JT
0113 2331955

Psychosynthesis and Education
  Trust
90/92 Tooley Street
London SE1 2TH
0171 403 2100

Westminster Pastoral Foundation
Training Department
23 Kensington Square
London W8 5HN
0171 937 6956

References

Adam, B. (1992) 'Time and health implicated: a conceptual critique', in R. Frankenberg (ed.), *Time, Health and Medicine*. London: Sage.

Adam, B. (1995) *Timewatch: The Social Analysis of Time*. Cambridge: Polity.

Aguilera, D.C. (1990) *Crisis Intervention: Theory and Methodology*, 7th edn. St. Louis, MO: Mosby.

Alexander, F. and French, T.M. (1946) *Psychoanalytic Therapy: Principles and Application*. New York: Ronald Press.

Andreas, S. and Andreas, C. (1992) 'Neuro-linguistic programming', in S.H. Budman, M.F. Hoyt and S. Friedman (eds), *The First Session in Brief Therapy*. New York: Guilford.

APA (1995) *Diagnostic and Statistical Manual of Mental Disorders*, 4th edn. Washington DC: American Psychiatric Association.

Aveline, M. (1995) 'Assessing the value of brief intervention at the time of assessment for dynamic psychotherapy', in M. Aveline and D.A. Shapiro (eds), *Research Foundations for Psychotherapy Practice*. Chichester: Wiley.

Balint, M., Ornstein, P.O. and Balint, E. (1972) *Focal Psychotherapy*. London: Tavistock.

Barkham, M. (1990) 'Research in individual therapy', in W. Dryden (ed.) *Individual Therapy: A Handbook*. Milton Keynes: Open University Press.

Barkham, M. and Shapiro, D. (1990) 'Brief psychotherapeutic interventions for job-related distress: a pilot study of prescriptive and exploratory therapy', *Counselling Psychology Quarterly*, 3(2): 133–47.

Barten, H.H. (1971) *Brief Therapies*. New York: Behavioral Publications.

Baudrillard, J. (1994) *The Illusion of the End*. Cambridge: Polity.

Blackburn, I.M. and Davidson, K. (1990) *Cognitive Therapy for Depression and Anxiety*. Oxford: Blackwell.

Bond, T. (1993) *Standards and Ethics for Counselling in Action*. London: Sage.

Boscolo, L. and Bertrando, P. (1993) *The Times of Time: A New Perspective in Systemic Therapy and Consultation*. New York: Norton.

Brazier, D. (1995) *Zen Therapy*. London: Constable.

Brundage, D.H. and Mackeracher, D. (1980) *Adult Learning Principles and their Application to Program Planning*. Toronto: The Ontario Institute for Studies in Education.

Budman, S.H. (ed.) (1981) *Forms of Brief Therapy*. New York: Guilford.

Budman, S.H. and Gurman, A.S. (1988) *Theory and Practice of Brief Therapy*. London: Hutchinson.

Budman, S.H., Hoyt, M.F. and Friedman, S. (eds) (1992) *The First Session in Brief Therapy*. New York: Guilford.

Burns, D. (1990) *The Feeling Good Handbook*. New York: Plume.

Cade, B. and O'Hanlon, W.H. (1993) *A Brief Guide to Brief Therapy*. New York: Norton.

Carlson, R. (1995) *Shortcut Through Therapy*. New York: Plume.

Castelnuovo-Tedesco, P. (1986) *The Twenty-Minute Hour: A Guide to Brief Psychotherapy for the Physician*. Washington, DC: American Psychiatric Press.

Chaplin, J. (1988) *Feminist Counselling in Action*. London: Sage.

Clarkson, P. (1995) *The Therapeutic Relationship*. London: Whurr.

Cooper, J.F. (1995) *A Primer of Brief Psychotherapy*. New York: Norton.

Coren, A. (1996) 'Brief therapy – base metal or pure gold?', *Psychodynamic Counselling*, 2(1): 22–38.

Coveney, P. and Highfield, R. (1991) *The Arrow of Time*. London: Flamingo.

Cowmeadow, P. (1995) 'Very brief psychotherapeutic interventions with deliberate self-harmers', in A. Ryle (ed.), *Cognitive Analytic Therapy: Developments in Theory and Practice*. Chichester: Wiley.

Crits-Cristoph, P. and Barber, J. (eds) (1991) *Handbook of Short-term Dynamic Therapies*. New York: Basic Books.

Cummings, A., Barak, A. and Hallberg, E.T. (1995) 'Session helpfulness and session evaluation in short-term counselling', *Counselling Psychology Quarterly*, 8(4): 325–32.

Cummings, N.A. (1988) 'Emergence of the mental health complex: adaptive and maladaptive responses', *Professional Psychology: Research and Practice*, 19(3): 308–15.

Cummings, N.A. (1990a) 'Arguments for the financial efficacy of psychological services in health care settings', in J.J. Sweet et al. (eds), *Handbook of Clinical Psychology in Medical Settings*. New York: Plenum.

Cummings, N.A. (1990b) 'Brief intermittent psychotherapy throughout the life cycle', in J.K. Zeig and S.G. Gilligan (eds), *Brief Therapy: Myths, Methods and Metaphors*. New York: Brunner/Mazel.

Cummings, N.A. and Sayama, M. (1995) *Focused Psychotherapy: A Casebook of Brief, Intermittent Psychotherapy Throughout the Life Cycle*. New York: Brunner/Mazel.

Cunningham, G. (1994) *Effective Employee Assistance Programs: A Guide for EAP Counselors and Managers*. Thousand Oaks, CA: Sage.

Curran, A. and Higgs, R. (1993) 'Setting up a counsellor in primary care: the evolution and experience in one general practice', in R. Corney and R. Jenkins (eds), *Counselling in General Practice*. London: Routledge.

Curtis, J.M. (1981) 'Determinants of the therapeutic bond: how to engage clients', *Psychological Reports*, 49: 415–19.

Dartington, A. (1995) 'Very brief psychodynamic counselling with young people', *Psychodynamic Counselling*, 1(2): 253–61.

Davanloo, H. (1990) *Unlocking the Unconscious*. Chichester: Wiley.

de Shazer, S. (1991) *Putting Difference to Work*. New York: Norton.

Deurzen-Smith, E. van (1988) *Existential Counselling in Practice*. London: Sage.

Dinnage, R. (1989) *One to One: Experiences of Psychotherapy*. Harmondsworth: Penguin.

Doktor, D. (1996) 'Being together briefly: one-on-one brief dramatherapy with clients hospitalized for chronic or reactive depression', in A. Gersie (ed.), *Dramatic Approaches to Brief Therapy*. London: Jessica Kingsley Publishers.

Dryden, W. (1991) *A Dialogue with Arnold Lazarus: 'It Depends'*. Buckingham: Open University Press.

Dryden, W. (1992) *The Dryden Interviews: Dialogues on the Psychotherapeutic Process*. London: Whurr.

Dryden, W. (1995) *Brief Rational Emotive Behaviour Therapy*. Chichester: Wiley.

Dryden, W. and Feltham, C. (1992) *Brief Counselling: A Practical Guide for Beginning Practitioners*. Buckingham: Open University Press.

Dryden, W. and Feltham, C. (1994) *Developing the Practice of Counselling*. London: Sage.

Egan, G. (1994) *The Skilled Helper*, 5th edn. Pacific Grove, CA: Brooks/Cole.

Ellis, A. (1996) *Better, Deeper and More Enduring Brief Therapy*. New York: Brunner/Mazel.

Elton Wilson, J. (1996) *Time-Conscious Psychological Therapy: A Life Stage to go Through*. London: Routledge.

Feltham, C. (1995) *What Is Counselling?: The Promise and Problem of the Talking Therapies*. London: Sage.

Flegenheimer, W.V. (1982) *Techniques of Brief Psychotherapy*. New York: Aronson.

Frances, A. and Clarkin, J.F. (1981) 'No treatment as the prescription of choice', *Archives of General Psychiatry*, 38: 542–5.

Frankl, V.E. (1973) *The Doctor and the Soul: From Psychotherapy to Logotherapy*. Harmondsworth: Pelican.

Frankl, V.E. (1985) *Psychotherapy and Existentialism: Selected Papers on Logotherapy*. New York: Washington Square Press.

Freeman, D. (1990) *Couples in Conflict*. Milton Keynes: Open University Press.

Freeman, D.R. (1968) 'Social work counselling – short-term crisis intervention', *Canadian Counsellor*, 2(1): 28–34.

Freud, S. (1985 [1920]) *On Metapsychology: The Theory of Psychoanalysis*. Harmondsworth: Pelican.

Garfield, S.L. (1989) *The Practice of Brief Psychotherapy*. Oxford: Pergamon.

Garfield, S.L. (1995) *Psychotherapy: An Eclectic-Integrative Approach*, 2nd edn. New York: Wiley.

Gersie, A. (ed.) (1996) *Dramatic Approaches to Brief Therapy*. London: Jessica Kingsley.

Gitlin, M. (1990) *Making Time Work For You: An Inner Guide To Time Management*. London: Sheldon.

Gold, J.R. and Wachtel, P.L. (1993) 'Cyclical psychodynamics', in J. Stricker and J.R. Gold (eds) *Comprehensive Handbook of Psychotherapy Integration*. New York: Plenum.

Goldsmith, J. (1965) *Living Now*. New York: Citadel.

Goss, S. (1995) *The Value of Listening: The Final Evaluative Report on the Effec-*

tiveness of the Advice, Support and Counselling Unit of Lothian Regional Council Education Department. Glasgow: Strathclyde University Counselling Unit.

Graham, H. (1990) *Time, Energy and the Psychology of Healing.* London: Jessica Kingsley.

Grant, R., Mohamed, C. and Smith, R. (1993) *Time Limited Psychotherapy at the Women's Therapy Centre: A Guide to Practice.* London: Women's Therapy Centre.

Gray, A. (1994) *An Introduction to the Therapeutic Frame.* London: Routledge.

Greenberg, R.P. and Bornstein, R.F. (1989) 'Length of psychiatric hospitalization and oral dependency', *Journal of Personality Disorders*, 3(3): 199–204.

Grinker, R.R. and Spiegel, J.P. (1944) 'Brief psychotherapy in war neuroses', *Psychosomatic Medicine*, 6: 123–31.

Groddeck, G. (1951) *The Unknown Self.* New York: Funk and Wagnalls.

Gustafson, J.P. (1986) *The Complex Secret of Brief Psychotherapy.* New York: Norton.

Haley, J. (1978) *Problem Solving Therapy.* New York: Harper and Row.

Hall, A. and Crisp, A.H. (1987) 'Brief psychotherapy in the treatment of anorexia nervosa: outcome at one year', *British Journal of Psychiatry*, 151: 185–91.

Happold, F.C. (1963) *Mysticism: A Study and an Anthology.* Harmondsworth: Pelican.

Harp, D. (1990) *The 3 Minute Meditator.* London: Piatkus.

Hawking, S. (1988) *A Brief History of Time.* London: Bantam.

Healy, D. (1990) *The Suspended Revolution: Psychiatry and Psychotherapy Re-examined.* London: Faber & Faber.

Herman, J.L. and Schatzow, E. (1984) 'Time-limited group therapy for women with a history of incest', *International Journal of Group Psychotherapy*, 34(4): 605–16.

Hobson, R.F. (1985) *Forms of Feeling: The Heart of Psychotherapy.* London: Tavistock.

Holloway, E. (1995) *Clinical Supervision: A Systems Approach.* Thousand Oaks, CA: Sage.

Holmes, J. and Lindley, R. (1989) *The Values of Psychotherapy.* Oxford: Oxford University Press.

Horowitz, M., Marmar, C., Krupnick, J., Wilner, N., Kaltreider, N. and Wallerstein, R. (1984) *Personality Styles and Brief Psychotherapy.* New York: Basic Books.

Howard, K.I., Kopta, S.M., Krause, M.S. and Orlinsky, D.E. (1986) 'The dose-response relationship in psychotherapy', *American Psychologist*, 41: 159–64.

Howe, D. (1989) *The Consumer's View of Family Therapy.* Aldershot: Gower.

Hunter, M. (1994) *Counselling in Obstetrics and Gynaecology.* Leicester: BPS Books.

James, T. and Woodsmall, W. (1988) *Time Line Therapy and the Basis of Personality.* Capitola, CA: Meta Publications Inc.

Jones, E.E., Cumming, J.D. and Horowitz, M.J. (1988) 'Another look at the non-specific hypothesis of therapeutic effectiveness', *Journal of Consulting and Clinical Psychology*, 56(1): 48–55.

Joseph, S., Williams, R. and Yule, W. (1993) 'Changes in outlook following disaster.

The preliminary development of a measure to assess positive and negative responses', *Journal of Traumatic Stress*, 6: 271–9.

Karasu, T.B. (1992) *Wisdom in the Practice of Psychotherapy*. New York: Basic Books.

Koss, M.P. and Butcher, J.N. (1986) 'Research on brief psychotherapy', in S.L. Garfield and A.E. Bergin (eds), *Handbook of Psychotherapy and Behavior Change*, 3rd edn. New York: Wiley.

Kottler, J.A. (1993) *On Being A Therapist*. San Francisco, CA: Jossey-Bass.

Kramer, P.D. (1989) *Moments of Engagement: Intimate Psychotherapy in a Technological Age*. New York: Norton.

Krishnamurti, J. and Bohm, D. (1985) *The Ending of Time*. London: Gollancz.

Lambert, M.J. (1992) 'Psychotherapy outcome research: implications for integrative and eclectic therapists', in J.C. Norcross and M.R. Goldfried (eds), *Handbook of Psychotherapy Integration*. New York: Basic Books.

Lazarus, A.A. (1958) 'New methods of psychotherapy: a case study', *South African Medical Journal*, 32: 660–4.

Lazarus, A.A. (1968) 'Learning theory and the treatment of depression', *Behaviour Research and Therapy*, 6: 83–9.

Lazarus, A.A. (1987) 'When more is better', in W. Dryden (ed.), *Key Cases in Psychotherapy*. London: Croom Helm.

Lazarus, A.A. (1989) *The Practice of Multimodal Therapy: Systemic, Comprehensive and Effective Psychotherapy*. Baltimore, MA: Johns Hopkins University Press.

Lazarus, A.A. and Fay, A. (1990) 'Brief psychotherapy: tautology or oxymoron?', in J.K. Zeig and S.G. Gilligan (eds), *Brief Therapy: Myths, Methods and Metaphors*. New York: Brunner/Mazel.

Lazarus, A.A., Glat, M. and Hassan, C.S. (1991) 'Multimodal therapy: a brief outline and two case histories', in K.N. Anchor (ed.), *Handbook of Medical Psychotherapy: Cost Effective Strategies in Mental Health*. Toronto: Hogrefe & Huber.

Macnab, F. (1993) *Brief Psychotherapy: An Integrative Approach in Clinical Practice*. Chichester: Wiley.

Mahrer, A.R. (1988) 'The briefest psychotherapy', *Changes*, 6(3): 86–9.

Malan, D.H. (1963) *A Study of Brief Psychotherapy*. London: Plenum.

Malan, D.H. (1976) *The Frontier of Brief Psychotherapy*. New York: Plenum.

Mann, J. (1973) *Time-Limited Psychotherapy*. Cambridge, MA: Harvard University Press.

Maple, F.F. (1985) *Dynamic Interviewing*. Newbury Park, CA: Sage.

Marks, I. (1989) 'Agoraphobia and panic disorder', in R. Baker (ed.), *Panic Disorder: Theory, Research and Practice*. Chichester: Wiley.

Marteau, L. (1986) *Existential Short Term Therapy*. London: Dympna Centre.

McCann, D.L. (1992) 'Post-traumatic stress disorder due to devastating burns overcome by a single session of eye movement desensitization', *Journal of Behavior Therapy and Experimental Psychiatry*, 23(4): 319–23.

McCord, J. (1978) 'A thirty-year follow-up study of treatment effects', *American Psychologist*, 33: 284–9.

McCormick, E. (1990a) *Change for the Better*. London: Unwin.

McCormick, E. (1990b) 'Cognitive analytic therapy in private practice', in A. Ryle (ed.), *Cognitive-Analytic Therapy: Active Participation in Change*. Chichester: Wiley.

McGrath, J.E. and Kelly, J.R. (1986) *Time and Human Interaction: Towards a Social Psychology of Time*. New York: Guilford.

Miller, W.R. and Rollnick, S. (1991) *Motivational Interviewing: Preparing People to Change Addictive Behavior*. New York: Guilford Press.

Miller, W.R., Taylor, C.A. and West, J.C. (1980) 'Focused versus broad-spectrum behaviour therapy for problem drinking', *Journal of Consulting and Clinical Psychology*, 48: 590–601.

Mohamed, C. and Smith, R. (1996) 'Time limited psychotherapy, in M. Maguire and M. Lawrence (eds), *Psychotherapy with Women*. London: Macmillan.

Molnos, A. (1995) *A Question of Time: Essentials of Brief Dynamic Psychotherapy*. London: Karnac.

Morss, J. (1995) *Growing Critical: Alternatives to Developmental Psychology*. London: Routledge.

Newman, F. (1991) *The Myth of Psychology*. New York: Castillo.

Nichols, M.P. (1974) 'Outcome of brief cathartic psychotherapy', *Journal of Consulting and Clinical Psychology*, 42(3): 403–10.

O'Hanlon, W.H. (1990) 'A grand unified theory for brief therapy: putting problems in context', in J.K. Zeig and S.G. Gilligan (eds), *Brief Therapy: Myths, Methods and Metaphors*. New York: Brunner/Mazel.

Older, J. (1977) 'Four taboos that may limit the success of psychotherapy', *Psychiatry*, 40: 197–204.

Oldfield, S. (1983) *The Counselling Relationship*. London: Routledge & Kegan Paul.

Palmer, S. and Dryden, W. (1995) *Counselling for Stress Problems*. London: Sage.

Patten, M.I. and Walker, L.G. (1990) 'Marriage guidance counselling; what clients think will help', *British Journal of Guidance and Counselling*, 18(1): 28–39.

Peake, T.H., Borduin, C.M. and Archer, R.P. (1988) *Brief Psychotherapies: Changing Frames of Mind*. Newbury Park, CA: Sage.

Pekarik, G. and Finney-Owen, G.K. (1987) 'Psychotherapists' attitudes and beliefs relevant to client drop-out', *Community Mental Health Journal*, 23(2): 120–30.

Perry, S. (1989) 'Treatment time and the borderline patient: an underappreciated strategy', *Journal of Personality Disorders*, 3(3): 230–9.

Pollin, I. (1995) *Medical Crisis Counseling: Short-Term Therapy for Long-Term Illness*. New York: Norton.

Premack, D. (1970) 'Mechanisms of self-control', in W.A. Hunt (ed.), *Learning Mechanisms in Smoking*. Chicago, IL: Aldine.

Preston, J., Varzos, N. and Liebert, D. (1995) *Every Session Counts: Making the Most of Your Brief Therapy*. San Luis Obispo, CA: Impact.

Pugh, L. (1992) 'Brief interventions in anticipatory grief and bereavement', *Counselling*, 3(1): 34–6.

Rawlence, C. (ed.) (1985) *About Time*. London: Jonathan Cape.

Rawson, P. (1992) 'Focal and short-term psychotherapy is a treatment of choice', *Counselling*, 3(2): 106–7.

Redfearn, J. (1992) *The Exploding Self: The Creative and Destructive Nucleus of the Personality*. Wilmette, IL: Chiron.

Regan, A.M. and Hill, C.E. (1992) 'Investigation of what clients and counselors do not say in brief therapy', *Journal of Counseling Psychology*, 39(2): 168–74.

Resick, P.A. and Mechanic, M.B. (1995) 'Brief cognitive therapies for rape victims', in A.R. Roberts (ed.), *Crisis Intervention and Time-Limited Cognitive Treatment*. Thousand Oaks, CA: Sage.

Reynolds, D. (1985) *Playing Ball on Running Water*. London: Sheldon.

Robertiello, R.C. and Schoenewolf, G. (1987) 101 *Common Therapeutic Blunders: Countertransference and Counterresistance in Psychotherapy*. Northvale, NJ: Aronson.

Roberts, A.R. (ed.) (1995a) *Crisis Intervention and Time-Limited Cognitive Treatment*. Thousand Oaks, CA: Sage.

Roberts, A.R. (1995b) 'Crisis intervention units and centers in the United States', in A.R. Roberts (ed.), *Crisis Intervention and Time-Limited Cognitive Treatment*. Thousand Oaks, CA: Sage.

Rogers, C.R. and Dymond, F. (1954) *Psychotherapy and Personality Change*. Chicago, IL: University of Chicago Press.

Rosen, B. (1990) 'Brief focal psychotherapy', in S. Bloch (ed.), *An Introduction to the Psychotherapies*, 2nd edn. Oxford: Oxford University Press.

Rowan, J. (1993a) 'Counselling for a brief period', in W. Dryden (ed.), *Questions and Answers on Counselling in Action*. London: Sage.

Rowan, J. (1993b) *The Transpersonal: Psychotherapy and Counselling*. London: Routledge.

Rowe, D. (1994) *Time On Our Side*. London: HarperCollins.

Rusk, T. (1991) *Instead of Therapy*. Carson, CA: Hay House.

Rycroft, C. (1972) *A Critical Dictionary of Psychoanalysis*. Harmondsworth: Penguin.

Ryle, A. (1990) *Cognitive-Analytic Therapy: Active Participation in Change*. Chichester: Wiley.

Ryle, A. (ed.) (1995) *Cognitive Analytic Therapy: Developments in Theory and Practice*. Chichester: Wiley.

Scott, M.J. and Dryden, W. (1996) 'The cognitive–behavioural paradigm', in R. Woolfe and W. Dryden (eds), *Handbook of Counselling Psychology*. London: Sage.

Seligman, M.E.P. (1975) *Helplessness: On Depression, Development and Death*. San Francisco, CA: Freeman.

Shallis, M. (1983) *On Time*. Harmondsworth: Pelican.

Shapiro, F. (1995) *Eye Movement Desensitisation and Reprocessing: Basic Principles, Protocols and Procedures*. New York: Guilford.

Sifneos, P.E. (1972) *Short-Term Psychotherapy and Emotional Crisis*. Cambridge, MA: Harvard University Press.

Sledge, W.H., Moras, K., Hartley, D. and Levine, M.A. (1990) 'Effects of time-limited psychotherapy on patient drop-out rates', *American Journal of Psychiatry*, 147(10): 1342–7.

Slife, B.D. (1993) *Time and Psychological Explanation*. New York: State University of New York Press.

Smith, M.L., Glass, G.V. and Miller, T.I. (1980) *The Benefits of Psychotherapy*. Baltimore, MA: The Johns Hopkins University Press.

Snow, S. (1996) 'Focusing on mythic imagery in brief dramatherapy with psychotic individuals', in A. Gersie (ed.), *Dramatic Approaches to Brief Therapy*. London: Jessica Kingsley.

Sterba, R.F. (1951) 'A case of brief psychotherapy of Sigmund Freud', *Psychoanalytic Review*, 38: 75–80.

Striano, J. (1988) *Can Psychotherapists Hurt You?*. Santa Barbara, CA: Professional Press.

Stroebe, M.S., Stroebe, W. and Hansson, R.O. (eds) (1993) *Handbook of Bereavement: Theory, Research and Intervention*. Cambridge: Cambridge University Press.

Strupp, H.H. (1990) 'Time-limited dynamic psychotherapy: development and implementation of a training program', in J.K. Zeig and S.G. Gilligan (eds), *Brief Therapy: Myths, Methods and Metaphors*. New York: Brunner/Mazel.

Sue, D.W. and Sue, D. (1990) *Counseling the Culturally Different: Theory and Practice*, 2nd edn. New York: Wiley.

Talmon, M. (1990) *Single Session Therapy: Maximising the Effect of the First (and Often Only) Therapeutic Encounter*. San Francisco, CA: Jossey-Bass.

Tedeschi, R.G. and Calhoun, L.G. (1995) *Trauma and Transformation: Growing in the Aftermath of Suffering*. Thousand Oaks, CA: Sage.

Thomas, B. (1991) *The Body of Time*. London: Arkana.

Thorne, B. (1994) 'Brief companionship', in D. Mearns, *Developing Person-Centred Counselling*. London: Sage.

Van Bilsen, H.P.J.G. (1996) *Treating Addictive Behaviours: A Manual of Brief Therapy for Addictions*. Chichester: Wiley.

Weiss, J. and Sampson, H. (1986) *The Psychoanalytic Process: Theory, Clinical Observations and Empirical Research*. New York: Guilford.

Wells, R.A. and Gianetti, V.J. (eds) (1990) *Handbook of the Brief Psychotherapies*. New York: Plenum.

Whitrow, G.J. (1988) *Time in History: The Evolution of Our General Awareness of Time and Temporal Perspective*. Oxford: Oxford University Press.

Williams, D. (1994) 'To the point', *Counselling News*, 13: 3–4.

Wilson, T. (1981) 'Behavior therapy as a short-term therapeutic approach', in S.H. Budman (ed.), *Forms of Brief Therapy*. New York: Guilford Press.

Wolberg, L.R. (1965) *Short-Term Psychotherapy*. New York: Grune & Stratton.

Woolger, R.J. (1990) *Other Lives, Other Selves: A Jungian Psychotherapist Discovers Past Lives*. Wellingborough: Crucible.

Worden, J.W. (1991) *Grief Counselling and Grief Therapy: A Handbook for the Mental Health Practitioner*, 2nd edn. London: Tavistock/Routledge.

Zeig, J.K. and Gilligan, S.G. (eds) (1990) *Brief Therapy: Myths, Methods and Metaphors*. New York: Brunner/Mazel.

Zirkle, G.A. (1961) 'Five-minute psychotherapy', *American Journal of Psychiatry*, 2(118): 544–6.

Index